EVERYTHING YOU NEED TO KNOW BEFORE YOU'RE 16

(But Won't Get Taught in School)

100+ Essential Life Skills for Self-Confidence, Happiness, and Success

FERNE BOWE

ISBN: 978-1-915833-54-9

View all our books at **bemberton.com**

CONTENTS

CONTENTS

INTRODUCTION

Welcome to one of the most exciting chapters of your life! Whether you've picked up this book out of curiosity or had it handed to you by a well-meaning adult, one thing is certain: you're in the midst of the whirlwind that is the teenage years.

Did you know that at 16, in some countries, you can legally marry, drive a car, or get a full-time job? These are huge milestones that come with some serious responsibilities. And yet, many teens are thrown into adulthood without having the real-life skills to navigate these challenges. Schools often focus on subjects like algebra, history, and geography, which are all well and good, but they often skip over the skills that truly build confidence and self-esteem.

Your teen years are filled with "firsts." Meeting new friends, taking big tests, and figuring out who you are — all these experiences shape the person you'll become as you step into adulthood. You'll make mistakes, sure, but those are just stepping stones to learning and growth.

That's where this book comes in — your ultimate guide to mastering the essential life skills that school doesn't teach. It's designed to help you make the most of these transformative years by providing practical knowledge to handle whatever life throws your way. Inside, you'll discover how to:

- **Boost your self-confidence**
- **Set goals and achieve your dreams**
- **Embrace mistakes and bounce back stronger**
- **Build and maintain strong friendships**
- **Handle crushes, relationships, and heartache**
- **Navigate social media and digital communication**

Feel free to jump around the chapters based on what interests you the most or what you need help with right now. Each section is packed with practical advice and relatable examples to guide you on your journey. **This book is your companion — write in it, highlight it, and make it truly yours.**

As you explore these pages, keep an open mind and be ready to learn and try new things. There might be some sections that aren't for you, and that's perfectly okay. Take the advice that resonates with you and leave the rest. Having an open, curious mind is a life skill in itself, so this book is a great place to start practicing.

Being a teenager can feel overwhelming at times, but it's also a unique opportunity for exploration and growth. This is your time to take risks, learn from mistakes, and embrace new experiences. Use this book as your guide to navigate these exciting years. Let it help you discover your strengths and passions as you become the person you're meant to be.

BEMBERTON
BOOKS

SOMETHING
FOR YOU

Thanks for buying this book. To show our appreciation, here's a **FREE** printable copy of the "Life Skills for Tweens Workbook"

WITH OVER 80 FUN ACTIVITIES JUST FOR TWEENS!

Scan the code to download your FREE printable copy

1

SELF-CONFIDENCE — YOU ARE AMAZING!

"Low self-confidence isn't a life sentence. Self-confidence can be learned, practiced, and mastered, just like any other skill. Once you master it, everything in your life will change for the better."
— Barrie Davenport

Have you ever felt you could take on the world? Maybe it was after acing a test, winning a game, or simply having a great day.

That feeling is self-confidence — believing in your abilities and feeling good about yourself. But self-confidence isn't a given. Sometimes, feeling at home in your skin and surroundings is tricky. Fortunately, as Barrie Davenport says, self-confidence is a skill you can learn and practice. Your confidence in yourself will see you through the challenging teen years and help you thrive.

This chapter is all about self-confidence and learning about your unique personal strengths. It will explain how you can fan the flame of your self-confidence by overcoming self-doubt and skipping the negative self-talk. By the end of the chapter, you'll be ready to embrace the things that make you different. You will also understand how confidence comes from making mistakes and stepping out of your comfort zone.

What Is Self-Confidence?

Self-confidence is trust in yourself and your abilities. It's the feeling that you're capable and worthy. Self-confidence allows you to take on challenges, like trying out for the school play or learning to play a musical instrument. More than that, confidence helps you embrace your unique strengths and quirks.

DID YOU KNOW? Confident people are often quiet. They don't feel like they have to prove anything, because the only person whose opinion matters is their own.

Why Is Self-Confidence Important?

Do you have big dreams for your life? Self-confidence is what helps you get there.

Anyone who has achieved something remarkable has had to leap out of their comfort zone, make mistakes, and grow. Doing big, scary things means you have to back yourself.

- **Self-confidence makes you resilient.** It lets you bounce back from challenges and setbacks. Instead of seeing your mistakes as personal shortcomings, you learn from them.
- **Self-confidence makes you gritty.** (This sounds gross, but it's the magic sauce for success.) We'll discuss grit and growth mindset later in the chapter, because they're juicy topics.
- **Self-confidence makes you courageous enough to get out of your comfort zone.** When you trust your abilities, you're more likely to pursue your goals and take action. That may mean speaking up in class or trying out for a sports team.
- **When you're self-confident, you love yourself.** You don't compare yourself to others. Instead, you feel content with the person you are — unique quirks and all.

At its core, self-confidence is about accepting and valuing yourself and your abilities. It helps you see all the qualities that make you special and uniquely you!

Celebrating Your Unique Qualities

Are you kind? Does algebra excite you? Can you talk your way out of any problem?

We all have skills and abilities that make us who we are. Self-confidence is about learning to embrace your quirks and talents.

WHAT IS A PERSONAL STRENGTH?

Personal strengths are the qualities and abilities that make you who you are. They could be:

- **Intellectual:** Like being great at math
- **Emotional:** Like having empathy
- **Creative:** Like playing an instrument
- **Physical:** Like being good at track

Your strengths are the gifts and personality traits that help you navigate challenges, work towards goals, and thrive.

- **Character-Based Strengths:** Sometimes, personal strengths are based on your character. These are your moral values, such as honesty, integrity, and compassion. These personal strengths help you make good choices.
- **Talents and Skills:** Other times, your strengths are based on your abilities and skills. For example, you might have a good

ear for music. However, it is important to remember that your ability to play the piano comes from developing your talent through hard work and practice.

- **Interpersonal Skills:** Finally, some personal strengths are based on interpersonal skills. Empathy, communication, and teamwork can improve relationships and make you a good leader.

WHY EMBRACING YOUR PERSONAL STRENGTHS IS IMPORTANT

When you embrace your strengths, you can leverage them. This transitional time can be tough when you're no longer a child but also not yet an adult. But your strengths can help you feel confident and empowered as you navigate the journey of finding who you are. Your strengths help you push boundaries, make decisions, and deal with change. When you see your differences as strengths, a whole world of opportunity opens up.

- **Self-Discovery:** Embracing all the parts of yourself helps you learn who you are. You can explore what you do and don't like and what's important to you.
- **Authenticity:** Why would you want to be someone else when you can be you? Embracing your strengths helps you celebrate what makes you different. Being authentic lets you feel confident in your individuality rather than conforming to fit in.

- **Happiness:** Think about the times you've felt unhappy. How many of them have been because of what others made you think? When you embrace your quirks and love who you are, other people's opinions don't matter. Celebrating your individuality, hobbies, and passions will make you feel happier and more content.

Discovering Your Strengths with a "Strengths" Map

Have you ever stopped to consider your strengths? You probably have a long list of weaknesses, but part of developing self-confidence is recognizing all your amazing qualities. A "strengths" map is an easy, fun way to acknowledge your passions, interests, and abilities. Your map can be physical (like a poster) or digital.

- **List Your Natural Talents:** Write down all your natural talents and abilities. Maybe you sing beautifully or have fantastic ball skills.
- **Recognize Developed Strengths:** Write down the strengths you have worked hard to develop, such as learning to code or mastering public speaking.
- **Include Fulfilling Activities:** Include the things that make you feel fulfilled and happy. For example, maybe you walk dogs at the shelter on weekends or love to spend hours immersed in a book.

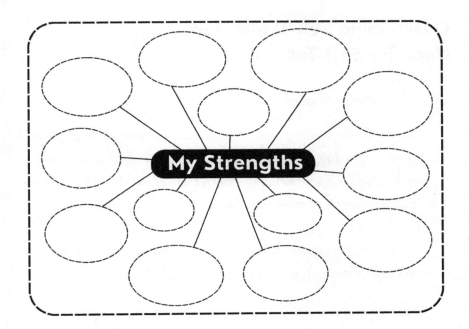

My Strengths

Top Tip

If you aren't sure what to write on your strengths map, ask your friends and family. They may notice strengths you haven't considered.

Overcoming Self-Doubt and Negative Self-Talk

Consider these two scenarios:

Sarah loves writing and dreams of becoming a published author one day. However, when her English teacher announces a writing competition, she doesn't enter. Rather than take a chance, Sarah worries that her writing isn't good enough.

Alex gets a lower grade than expected on a math test. He tells himself, "I'm so stupid. I'll never be good at math."

WHAT IS SELF-DOUBT AND NEGATIVE SELF-TALK?

Can you spot the self-doubt and negative self-talk in the above examples? Maybe it's familiar because you do it, too.

Self-doubt is a lack of confidence in your abilities. It can make you feel insecure and inadequate, like you're not enough.

Negative self-talk goes hand in hand with self-doubt. If you've ever criticized or talked badly about your body or character traits, you've experienced negative self-talk firsthand.

WHY ARE SELF-DOUBT AND NEGATIVE SELF-TALK A PROBLEM?

When you aren't confident in who you are and speak badly about yourself, it impacts every aspect of your life. You'll:

- Hesitate before making decisions.
- Look for approval from others.
- Avoid challenges and new opportunities.
- Catastrophize and blow things out of proportion.

DID YOU KNOW?

Negative self-talk increases stress levels and makes it harder to stay motivated and achieve goals.

CHALLENGING NEGATIVE SELF-TALK

Your brain is growing and changing, which is excellent news! A flexible brain means you can train it to stop negativity and rewire more positive pathways that become your brain's default setting.

Start a Thought Journal

One way to combat negative self-talk is to start a thought journal. When you write down your thoughts, you can monitor them and look for patterns of negativity. In order to make positive changes, you first have to identify the problems.

Example Thought Journal Entry:

Date: March 26, 2024

Situation (Who, What, When, Where):
At dinner, I fought with my dad about which subjects I wanted to study. He thinks he knows what is best but doesn't consider my feelings. What started as a discussion turned into a shouting match.

Emotion and Rating:
I feel angry, sad, frustrated, and unheard. 7/10

Immediate Thoughts:
My dad doesn't care what I want or what'll make me happy. I'm a terrible daughter for shouting at him, and I'm probably not good enough to be a writer anyway.

Examining My Thoughts and Feelings:
I've had some time to cool off and realize I might have been more defensive than needed. My dad just wants what's best for me, and I should have been more firm and respectful when talking to him about the subjects I wanted to do. I can't expect him to treat me like an adult when I throw a tantrum.

Reframing My Thoughts and Feelings:
Instead of letting this argument drive a wedge between me and Dad, I can use it to show him that I can apologize and have a respectful conversation. It's a chance for us to have an honest discussion about boundaries.

Using this thought journal layout, you can easily spot the situations that cause a high emotion rating, both good and bad. You can also see if you keep reacting to the same situations or people. Finding the negative patterns helps you change them.

Challenge Negative Self-Talk with the "Stop" Technique

Letting negative thoughts run riot in your brain is never a good idea. But how can you stop them?

The process is easier than you think. When you have a negative thought, block it and replace it with something positive.

Use the 3 D's:

1. **Disrupt:** Stop the thought from taking over.
2. **Disarm:** Acknowledge the thought to take away its power.
3. **Dismiss:** Swap out the negative for a positive.

How do you stop a negative thought spiral? Come up with something to help you break the cycle. Maybe it's shouting **"STOP"** in your head or rubbing your earlobe. Choose something you can do that will become a positive habit for negative thoughts.

Negative thoughts can sometimes feel like going down a rabbit hole. You find yourself in a negative thought tunnel you can't find your way out of. So why not try reversing the rabbit hole effect? Instead of thinking of the worst-case scenario, think of the best. For example, "What if I don't make the team?" becomes "What if I do make the team?"

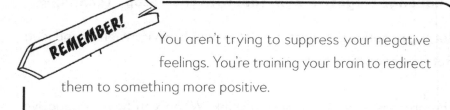

REMEMBER! You aren't trying to suppress your negative feelings. You're training your brain to redirect them to something more positive.

Cultivating Positive Affirmations

A positive affirmation is a short, specific hit of positivity that helps you feel confident and empowered. For example:

- "I am capable and strong."
- "I believe in my abilities and express my true self with ease."
- "I am deserving of success and happiness."

Why are positive affirmations so amazing?

- They keep you focused on your goals.
- They stop your negative self-talk.
- They help you foster a growth mindset.
- They're an easy way to remind yourself of your strengths.
- They help you reframe your weaknesses.

You can find a million different affirmations online, but writing your own allows you to personalize them to your goals.

Here's how:

- Make them about you! Start your affirmations with "I am," "I will," "I choose," or "I can."
- Where possible, keep them in the present tense. For example, "I am choosing to be patient today."
- Create an affirmation for each of your goals. The more specific and focused, the better.
- Keep them short. The goal is to say them regularly throughout the day, so quick and simple is best.
- Choose where you stick your affirmations. The bathroom mirror, above your desk, or beside your bed are all good spots.

Your positive affirmations should be part of your daily routine. You can say them while getting dressed in the morning or before you get out of bed. Saying them in the mirror can also be very powerful because you are saying them to yourself rather than just out loud.

Fostering Balanced Self-Perception

Recognizing and accepting your strengths is crucial for surviving the teenage years. But that doesn't mean you should stop challenging yourself to learn and grow. Having balanced self-perception means appreciating your strengths and working on your weaknesses. It's a realistic view of who you are without judgment, criticism, or negativity.

To be self-confident, you need to embrace all of you. Understanding that you are complex and unique helps you be authentically you!

Here's a quick exercise to start the process:

- Write down five strengths and five weaknesses.
- For each strength, write one thing you struggle with. For example, you might be good at math but find geometry more challenging than algebra.
- For each weakness, write one way you can improve. For example, if you lack patience, you can count to 10 slowly while breathing deeply.

This exercise helps you see your strengths realistically and take a positive approach to weaknesses. People sometimes have blind spots regarding their personalities, so ask someone you trust to be honest about how they experience you. Getting an outside opinion can give you a different view of yourself and help keep your perceptions balanced and positive.

Self-Assessment Worksheet

Step 1: Identify Your Strengths and Weaknesses

Write down five strengths:

Strength 1: _____

Strength 2: _____

Strength 3: _____

Strength 4: _____

Strength 5: _____

Step 2: Analyze Your Strengths

For each strength, write down one thing you struggle with:

Strength 1: _____

Struggle: _____

Strength 2: _____

Struggle: _____

Strength 3: _____

Struggle: _____

Step 3: Improve Your Weakness

For each weakness, write down one way you can improve:

Weakness 1: _____

Improvement: _____

Weakness 2: _____

Improvement: _____

Weakness 3: _____

Improvement: _____

Weakness 4: _____

Improvement: _____

Take your time to reflect on your strengths and weaknesses honestly. Think of specific struggles and improvements that are practical and achievable.

Use this worksheet regularly to track your progress and make adjustments as needed. For each weakness, write down one way you can improve:

Building Resilience Through Challenges

Resilience is one of the biggest strengths you can work to develop. Being resilient means you bounce back from challenges and can push through disappointment and discomfort. Life will throw you curveballs, but a resilient mindset will help you deal with them and use those curveballs as opportunities rather than setbacks.

CULTIVATING A GROWTH MINDSET

Did you know that a growth mindset is essential for developing grit? Grit is one of the key ingredients for confidence, happiness, and success. Grit is your ability to keep going when things get tough and work towards long-term goals.

Let's dive into the details of a growth mindset so you can start fostering yours.

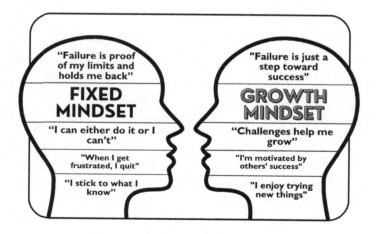

What Is a Growth Mindset?

Psychologist Carol Dweck believes people have either a growth or a fixed mindset.

If you have a **fixed mindset**, you:

- Believe your abilities can't be changed, and that they are "just who you are" (like the color of your eyes).
- Avoid challenges.
- Believe that success comes from talent, not hard work.
- Struggle to bounce back from challenges or failure.

If you have a **growth mindset**, you:

- Believe you can improve your abilities through hard work and consistent effort.
- Learn from your mistakes.
- See challenges as opportunities.
- Learn from feedback, both positive and negative.
- Focus on progress and effort.
- Are inspired by other peoples' successes, rather than threatened by them.

How to Recognize and Cultivate a Growth Mindset

You need a growth mindset, but how can you actually foster one?

To see this concept in action, list goals you haven't reached or things you see as weaknesses and turn them into "Yet" sentences.

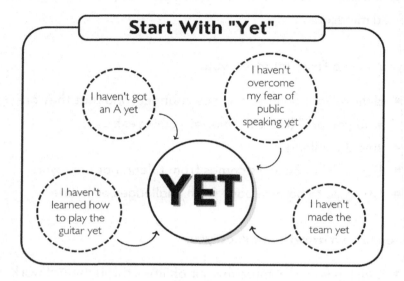

Try New Things

The easiest way to determine whether you have a fixed or growth mindset is to try new things. They don't need to be crazy or scary, but they should push you out of your comfort zone.

Here are some ideas to get you started:

- Try a new hobby, like painting or coding.
- Speak up during a class discussion.
- Join a club at school.

- Volunteer at your local community center.
- Get a part-time job.

Use Your Thought Journal

Go through your thought journal with two different-colored highlighters and find all the times you showed aspects of a fixed or growth mindset. Try to identify a pattern.

Make an effort to change the language you use in your journal entries. Whenever you write something negative, try and reframe it using words like "yet," "learn," "try," and "grow."

Find Joy In The Journey

Life can be uncomfortable, but part of having a growth mindset is learning to embrace discomfort and step out of your comfort zone. It's really where all the magic happens. When you achieve a goal, you're not uncomfortable anymore. Learn to enjoy the journey, because that is what helps you grow.

Learning from Past Challenges

Have you ever realized that you learn more from challenging situations and failure than success?

When you reflect constructively on past experiences, you can extract valuable lessons.

Create a "Challenge" Journal

Write down every time you encounter a challenging person, situation, or task.

Ask yourself:

- Why is this person, task, or situation challenging?
- How am I currently coping with this challenge?
- What are the potential outcomes or consequences if I don't address this challenge?
- What did I learn about myself?
- What skills or strengths did I develop due to overcoming this difficulty?
- How did this experience shape my perspective or values?
- What strategies or approaches have helped with similar challenges in the past?
- What would I do differently if faced with a similar challenge in the future?

A challenge journal helps you track what strategies are working. It allows you to see your growth as you learn to navigate tricky situations.

DREAMS AND PROJECTS

"A goal without a plan is just a wish."
— Antoine de Saint-Exupéry.

Have you ever considered that you can enjoy the fun times more when you have structure and goals to work towards?

Setting clear, attainable goals will help you achieve your goals and foster a growth mindset.

SMART Goals Framework

It's time to get serious about goal-setting. Your goals are probably different now than a few years ago, and bigger dreams require better planning. That's where the SMART goals framework comes in.

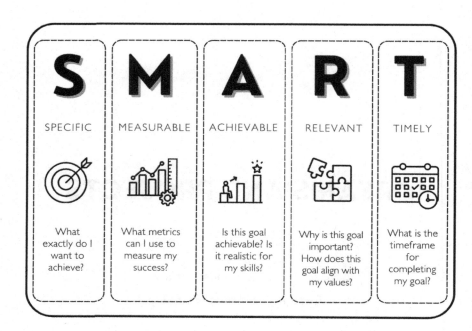

S-Specific

- What do I specifically want to accomplish?
- What do I want to achieve? What is the outcome of my goal?
- Can I clearly describe what success looks like for this goal?

M-Measurable

- How will I track my progress towards this goal?
- What metrics can I use to measure my success?
- How will I know when I have achieved my goal?

A–Achievable

- Is this goal realistic for my current circumstances and resources?
- What steps do I need to take to make this goal attainable?
- Do I have the necessary skills, knowledge, and support to achieve this goal?

R–Relevant

- Why is this goal important to me?
- How does this goal align with my values, interests, and long-term aspirations?
- What impact will achieving this goal have on my personal growth and development?

T–Time-Bound

- How much time am I willing to spend on this goal?
- What is the deadline or timeframe for completing this goal?
- What smaller milestones or checkpoints can I set to keep myself on track?

Here's an example of a SMART goal.

Goal: Improve my math grade

Specific: "I will improve my math grade from a C to a B by the end of the current semester."

Measurable: "I will track my progress by regularly reviewing my math assignments, quizzes, and tests. I will aim for a minimum score of 85% or higher on all math assessments."

Achievable: "I will achieve this goal by dedicating an extra hour each day to math study and practice. I will also get help from my math teacher or a tutor."

Relevant: "Improving my math grade is important to me because it will increase my overall GPA and open up more opportunities for college admissions and scholarships."

Time-Bound: "I will achieve this goal by the end of the current semester in 12 weeks. I will break down my study plan into weekly milestones and assess my progress to ensure I stay on track."

ALIGN YOUR GOALS WITH YOUR PASSIONS AND STRENGTHS

A secret to setting goals you'll actually work to achieve is aligning them with your strengths and passions. Do you need to work toward an A in math if you want to pursue a career as a journalist? Probably not. If this is the case, working toward a better math grade might be a challenging goal you struggle to stick to.

When your goals align with your values and things you consider important, you'll be more motivated and have a higher chance of success. For example, if making the track team aligns with your healthy lifestyle values, you are more likely to eat those leafy greens and make the early morning training sessions.

SELF-REFLECTION PRACTICES FOR MATCHING STRENGTHS WITH GOALS

It sounds cheesy, but bring your heart into the goal-setting process. Staying motivated is challenging when you set practical goals without an emotional element.

Journaling

Keep a journal and make it a habit to write down your thoughts, feelings, and experiences. Journaling is an excellent tool for identifying the activities, hobbies, and subjects that make you happy. Reflect on the activities you enjoy and what makes you lose track of time.

Over time, you will see patterns related to your happiest, most fulfilled moments. If you can tie your goals to those moments, you have a much higher chance of reaching them.

Reflective Prompts

If you want to take journaling one step further, try using open-ended questions and prompts to help you clarify your strengths and goals:

- Three things you are good at and love/enjoy.
- Three things you are good at but don't love/enjoy.
- Describe a time when you felt confident and capable.
- What skills or traits do you use to overcome challenges and obstacles?
- If you could do anything without limitations or fear of failing, what would it be? Why?
- What are you curious about? What is a topic you want to learn more about?

Mind-Mapping

If you prefer something more creative and visual, make a mind map. Write words, phrases, topics, and activities you love or want to achieve on a large board. Use drawing pins and string to create connections between areas that overlap.

Things I love, my dreams, what I want to achieve

Sometimes, having a visual roadmap of your interests and strengths can help you link them to your goals. You can also add things to your mind map, making it an evolving representation of your progress.

VISIBLE AND TOP-OF-MIND

Writing down your goals gives you clarity, keeps you committed, and offers accountability. It's like creating a map to help you reach them. A visual reminder of your goals lets you know what you want, where you are going, and the steps to take. When you write your goals down, you make a deal with yourself to follow through and make them happen.

Practical Tips for Displaying Your Goals

- **Use a Goal-Tracking App:** Apps allow you to take your goals with you. They have fun features like progress charts and reminders, and can also sync with your digital calendar.
- **Create a Vision Board:** A vision board is a powerful tool to help you visualize your goals and motivate you. Use colored pens, pictures, and quotes to create an inspirational roadmap for reaching your goals. You can also create a digital vision board for your phone or computer screensaver.
- **Keep Them Front and Center:** Stick your goals on the mirror and read them as you brush your teeth. Write your goals on paper, frame them, and place them beside your bed. Choose a word that reminds you of your progress in reaching your goals and put it on a keychain or piece of jewelry, or even print it onto a tote bag.

Breaking Down Goals Into Actionable Steps

Big goals can feel overwhelming, and feeling overwhelmed can prevent you from taking action. The best way to turn dreams into goals is to map out an action plan.

TECHNIQUES FOR PLANNING AND ORGANIZING TASKS

Benjamin Franklin said, "If you fail to plan, you are planning to fail." You won't magically achieve your goals without breaking them down into actionable steps you can take each day.

Planning helps you with the three C's of achieving your goals: Planning creates clarity, keeps you consistent, and increases your confidence.

Break Down Your Goals into Manageable Chunks

Start by breaking your goal into three to five steps. Then, break those steps into three to five smaller steps (or more, if needed.)

Example Goal: Get an A on the Math Final

Step 1: Assess My Weaknesses

- Review past quizzes, tests, and homework assignments to identify areas of weakness.
- Ask my teacher for feedback on specific topics or concepts that need improvement.
- Use online resources or textbooks to revisit challenging topics and fill in knowledge gaps.

Step 2: Develop a Study Plan

- Create a study schedule leading up to the final exam, allocating dedicated time each day for math review.
- Break down the material into manageable chunks, focusing on one topic or concept.
- Try different study techniques, such as practicing problems, creating flashcards, and finding a study buddy.

Step 3: Practice Regularly

- Set aside time each day for focused practice, working on a mix of problem-solving and concept reinforcement.
- Do one practice exam each week.
- Keep track of my progress and note areas that need extra focus.

Step 4: Get Support

- Set up a meeting with my teacher to review any concepts I still need help with.
- Form a study group two weeks before the final exam.

Step 5: Breaks and Rewards

- Decide on small rewards for completing tasks each week.
- Come up with fun break options that help take my mind off of math.

Tips and Tools

- **Be Realistic:** Write action items you can achieve in an hour or two. Short tasks are not only more realistic to complete, but also easier to schedule on a calendar.

- **Make It Easier:** If the chunks you have broken the goal into still feel overwhelming, make them smaller. It's your goal, so you can choose how you reach it. For example, if "Create a study schedule leading up to the final exam, allocating dedicated time each day for math review" feels stressful, break it down further:
  - Write down how many days/weeks you have until the final exam.
  - Write down all the sections or concepts you need to cover.
  - Assign each section a week.
  - Assign a subtopic to each day.
  - Write down what you will do within that subtopic (be specific), such as answering three practice questions or watching a YouTube tutorial explaining a concept.

Keep breaking down tasks until they feel achievable. The more confident you get, the easier it will be to tick tasks off your list.

- **Write Things Down:** Make a to-do list or use a planner to stay organized. Some people prefer a daily organizer, while others like a monthly calendar. If digital tools are more your thing, try a project management app. Just as writing your goals down keeps you accountable, daily tasks help you stay on track.

- **Declutter:** Keeping your space tidy can help you stay organized. When you have a space for everything, it's easy to find what you need when you need it. Organization also saves you time and energy. You can only review your notes if you know where they are. Try organizing your notes in color-coded folders or using specific Post-it notes for reminders.

Sometimes, your head needs decluttering, too. When your head feels scattered and your goals feel too big, get your journal out. Write down everything you're worried about, including your to-do list. Try something called "stream of consciousness" writing. Write down everything you think as you think it. This is an excellent technique for helping you work through a situation or emotions that are troubling you. Writing in your journal can help clear your mind, improving your focus as you work toward your goals.

THE IMPORTANCE OF DEADLINES AND TIMELINES

Deadlines help you get things done. Working hard and sticking to a strict schedule is easier when an end date is in sight. Deadlines hold you accountable. They are a commitment you make to yourself. Also, a sense of urgency can help you push through and do the work, even when you don't want to.

Did you know that there are different types of goals? There are long-term, short-term, realistic, and challenging goals. You need a balance of these types to stay motivated and gain confidence.

Long-Term Goals

Long-term goals take longer to achieve. They are challenging and don't offer an immediate payoff. For example:

- **A (Realistic) Long-Term Goal:** Get an A on the math final by the end of the semester.
- **A (Challenging) Long-Term Goal:** Maintain an A average in math class consistently throughout the semester.

Short-Term Goals

Short-term goals are generally more straightforward. They can boost your confidence and help motivate you as you work towards a bigger goal.

- **A (Realistic) Short-Term Goal:** Complete all my homework and practice problems for each chapter covered in class.
- **A (Challenging) Short-Term Goal:** Schedule regular study sessions for math at least three times a week, dedicating focused time to review and practice.

Tips

- **Always add buffer time to your timeline.**
- **Work backward from your deadline to ensure you have enough time for everything.**
- **Be realistic about how long tasks will take, bearing in mind your other responsibilities.**
- **Be honest with yourself about your bad habits.** Do you get caught up in scrolling for longer than you should? Or do you catch yourself saying, "Just one more chapter" when reading a book? Be aware of the habits that make time management tricky.

TIPS FOR STAYING ORGANIZED AND TRACKING YOUR PROGRESS

Remember how SMART goals need to be measurable? Tracking your progress helps you see what steps to take next, celebrate your wins, and change your plan.

How Can You Track Your Progress?

Determining which strategy works best to track your progress takes experimentation.

- **Visual Tracker:** Nothing helps keep you accountable and motivated like a visual representation of your progress and success. You can be as creative as you like with your visual tracker. For example, try a coloring page with different pictures for each task. Or, create a "goal tree" where you add a leaf for each task you complete.

- **Goal Puzzle:** Print your goal onto a puzzle template and cut out each piece. Every time you complete a task, add a piece to the puzzle until it's complete.
- **Sticker Chart:** Stickers are an easy way to customize your goal chart. Choose stickers for each goal and add them as you complete tasks.
- **Reward System:** Set up a reward system to stay motivated. Add a token to a jar each time you complete a task. At the end of the week, tally your tokens and get a reward based on how many you have. The more tokens you have, the better the reward. Ask your parents to help you with bigger rewards, like an extra allowance, a later curfew, or an outing with friends.

Why Should You Review Your Progress?

Breaking down goals and having a plan is one thing, but you must also regularly review your strategies and progress to see what is working.

Reviewing your progress has numerous benefits, including:

- Increased self-awareness.
- A chance to celebrate your successes.
- Learning from your mistakes.

- Assessing whether your goal is still important to you.
- Re-evaluating your timeline and deadline.

Goals and the process of reaching them should be flexible. Keep checking in with yourself to see what's working and eliminate the things that aren't.

Dealing with Setbacks and Staying Motivated

If reaching goals were easy, you wouldn't need to prep, plan, and track your progress. But that's the beauty of setting goals — the more you set, the better you get.

PERSEVERANCE AND RESILIENCE

Resilience and perseverance are essential as you face challenges and setbacks. Every day, ordinary people overcome adversity and hardships to do ordinary things in extraordinary ways. Let's learn about a few of them to help you stay motivated.

Inspirational Stories About Perseverance

Bethany Hamilton was attacked by a 14-foot tiger shark and lost her left arm at the age of 13. But rather than let the experience end her dreams of becoming a professional surfer, she was back in the water a month later. At 17, Bethany realized her dream of surfing professionally — and she still surfs today! Bethany didn't let tragedy stop her from achieving her dreams and doing what she loved, but it took enormous courage, resilience, and perseverance.

Bill Gates is a famed entrepreneur, but he wasn't always successful. He dropped out of Harvard, and his first company, Traf-O-data, failed after six years. Imagine if he hadn't been brave enough to try again. Microsoft would never have happened. By 31, Bill Gates was a self-made billionaire because he persevered and learned from his mistakes.

Jay-Z is one of the biggest names in the music industry. But did you know that he originally couldn't get signed? Instead of giving up his dream of making music, Jay-Z started his own record label. Not only did his Roc-a-Fella label sell millions of records, but he also branched out into other business ventures. Jay-Z didn't let his tough childhood in Brooklyn's Marcy Projects stop him from trying, failing, learning, and succeeding.

MISTAKES ARE FOR LEARNING

"Every failure is a step to success"
– William Whewell

Resilience is a muscle you strengthen whenever you embrace a challenge and get up when life knocks you down. Resiliency comes from doing hard things imperfectly. You aren't born with a resilient mindset; you learn it.

- **Validate your emotions:** Your feelings aren't good or bad; they just are. You might react badly to an emotion, but the emotion itself is a teaching tool. Accept your feelings and then let them go. If you hold on to anger, fear, and sadness, it will be harder to try again and move forward. A Feelings Wheel is a helpful tool for figuring out your feelings.

- **Get back on track:** Don't get stuck in what you "can't" do. Acknowledge your limitations, be kind to yourself, and keep moving forward. Having an action plan is a great way to always have something to refer back to when you get off track. A resilient mindset lets you see mistakes as learning opportunities so you can adjust your plan.

- **Have a positive outlook:** Don't take failure personally. This is easier said than done, of course. However, your failure doesn't define you, and it certainly doesn't say anything about who you are as a person. Imagine if Bill Gates or Jay-Z had taken their failures to mean they weren't good enough.

KEEP THAT MOTIVATION GOING

Motivation comes and goes. You need to find out what motivates you and create a strategy that gives you the edge to reach your goals. You need a mix of intrinsic and extrinsic motivation to keep you working toward your goals.

- **Intrinsic Motivation:** When you are intrinsically motivated, working toward your goal makes you happy and gives you a sense of satisfaction.

- **Extrinsic Motivation:** When you are extrinsically motivated, you complete tasks to get a reward.

- **Visualize yourself reaching your goal.** Picture in your mind what the moment will look and feel like. Be as detailed as possible. Visualization is extremely powerful. It helps you create a blueprint for success by actively creating the outcome you are trying to achieve.

- **Set rewards along the way.** Studying for the math final might be tedious, but you can keep things interesting. Have a treat jar that you can raid after a successful study session, or give yourself a night off if you study every day for a week. Link the rewards to the completion of specific tasks.

- **Get rid of negative influences.** You need friends and family who will motivate you to stay on track, not tempt you to get off track. Be open and honest with the people around you, explaining why your goal is important. Let them know that you want their support and encouragement. If your friends are harming you more than helping, talk to them about it. Negative influences can also include technology or distractions. Lock your phone away during study sessions and keep your space distraction-free.

Creating a Support System

Create a network of people you can depend on as you work toward your goals. This network can include friends, family, coaches, and mentors. Your support system will help keep you focused and motivated. It will also hold you accountable with kindness and love.

Surrounding yourself with the right people means you can ask for help when you need it. A support system lets you celebrate wins, share failures, and brainstorm solutions. They are the squad cheering you on when things get tough.

Your support system is invaluable, and it is important to show them your gratitude. Make time for them and be there to support them right back.

TIPS FOR ADJUSTING YOUR PLANS AND GOALS

Life happens, and sometimes, you need to adjust your plans and goals accordingly. Moving the goalposts is fine if you encounter unexpected obstacles or new information. A growth mindset is all about the ability to be flexible.

Simple Strategies for Adapting Your Goals and Plans

- **Regular reflection is essential:** You need to see what is and is not working before determining what needs to change.
- **Prioritize your goals:** You can't do everything all at once. If staying on top of tasks feels overwhelming, prioritize your goals and take some tasks off your plate.
- **Set new deadlines:** Adjust your timeline and set a new deadline. Reaching a goal should feel good, not exhausting.
- **Stay committed:** Changing the plan doesn't mean you should give it up. Simply adjust your timeline and strategies so they help you achieve your goal rather than hinder you.

Constructive self-reflection can help you learn from setbacks and apply the lessons to your plan. Examining yourself and your weaknesses can be difficult. However, try to treat setbacks with curiosity, not criticism. Consider what went wrong (and why) in a nonjudgmental way. You need to understand what went wrong to know where to go next. Setbacks aren't a problem — they are an opportunity for growth.

Focus on solutions, not problems!

3

FACING FAILURE

"You build on failure. You use it as a stepping stone. Close the door on the past. You don't try to forget the mistake, but you don't dwell on it. You don't let it have any of your energy, or any of your time, or any of your space."
– Johnny Cash

Failure is a part of life. Without it, you'll never grow into the person you're meant to be.

Here's an exercise that will show you why failure is important. Ask someone you respect and admire what helped them become who they are today. Chances are, their answer will involve failure. As it turns out, you learn more from failure than you do from success.

Consider this quote from Chris Hardwick: "No human ever became interesting by not failing. The more you fail and recover and improve, the better you are as a person. Ever meet someone who's always had everything work out for them with zero struggle? They usually have the depth of a puddle. Or they don't exist."

You don't want to have the depth of a puddle, do you?

Understanding Failure as a Part of Learning

Achieving anything, whether big or small, requires trial and error and failure. But don't think of failure as some big, awful thing. Instead, look at failure as a set of circumstances, and consider your reaction to them. You can either treat the situation as a disaster or find the lesson and move on.

Consider the story of Thomas Edison. Teachers at school told him that he was dumb. He had a hearing problem, which made classroom learning difficult. His mother pulled him out of school at age 11, and he began to teach himself in a way that made learning accessible. As an adult, Edison was an inventor who loved nothing more than creating things. But creativity requires failure. Edison failed thousands of times before inventing the first commercially viable lightbulb. He famously said, " I have not failed. I've just found 10,000 ways that won't work."

Abraham Lincoln is considered to be one of the greatest US Presidents. However, he had a rocky road that helped him become the man who would help end slavery. Lincoln had a limited education and mainly taught himself. Through grit and determination, he became a lawyer and a congressman. Before being elected president in 1860, Abraham Lincoln was defeated twice for nomination to Congress. He was also defeated for the US Senate twice and lost the nomination for vice-president.

Failure means you were brave enough to step out of your comfort zone. How you view failure will dictate how you respond to it. You will either learn, grow, and push through or stay stagnant (like a puddle).

Strategies for Constructive Self-Evaluation

Failure is a learning tool, but you must know how to use it. Failing is hard, but critically examining yourself can be even harder.

You have to separate your self-worth from your failure. Read that again.

Failure isn't the problem — your reaction to it is. When things go pear-shaped, it's easy to blame others or talk negatively about yourself, but self-criticism only makes you feel worse.

REMEMBER! Self-criticism increases procrastination, decreases motivation, and stops you from reaching your goals.

STRATEGIES FOR CONSTRUCTIVE SELF-CRITICISM

Self-criticism often stems from unrealistic expectations or worries about what other people think. But your worth doesn't come from your achievements, and you don't need to be good at everything.

NOBODY LOVES ME

I CAN'T DO IT

I'M NOT WORTHY

I'M NOT GOOD ENOUGH

I MUST NOT MAKE A MISTAKE

I MUST BE PERFECT

Criticize Specific Behaviors You Can Change

Focus on specific actions rather than generalizing about your abilities. For example, instead of saying, "I'm just stupid," try "I played video games instead of studying." This way, you can identify the behavior that needs to change.

Consider the Situation

Reflect on your actions. For example, if you played video games instead of studying because you didn't understand the concept, acknowledge that and plan to get extra help next time.

How Do Your Actions Affect Others?

Think about how your actions impact those around you. For example, your parents might be frustrated that you didn't ask for help.

Have a Self-Criticism Jar

Put a token in the jar every time you catch yourself using negative self-talk, and take a token out each time you view a setback or failure more positively. This can help you understand your thought patterns and encourage a more constructive mindset.

Tips for Feedback

When you have a support network, you can ask them for feedback. Sometimes, an outside perspective can offer you valuable insights.

- **Feedback doesn't have to be negative:** Respond with curiosity, not defensiveness.
- **Listen to understand:** Don't interrupt. Take a few minutes to process what is being said before responding.

- **Find the action item:** Sift through the feedback and use it to grow and do better.

Bounce Back with a Positive Mindset

A positive mindset is the tendency to be optimistic, even in the face of challenges. A positive attitude helps you accept the negative but look for the positive so you don't get stuck in a negative spiral. It also enables you to see the good in others.

WHY DO YOU NEED A POSITIVE MINDSET?

Positive thinking isn't just ignoring the bad stuff and pretending everything is okay. **A positive mindset helps you look for the positives and learning opportunities.** It allows you to accept reality, with the good, the bad, and everything in between. With a positive mindset, you can reject all-or-nothing thinking because life isn't all or nothing. It isn't black and white. It's a million shades of gray, filled with highs and lows.

Positivity gives you hope and helps you try again. It makes you feel grateful, even in the challenging moments.

Gratitude + Positivity = Happiness

Techniques for Maintaining Optimism

- **Gratitude Jar or Journal:** Every day, write three things you are grateful for in a journal or on a slip of paper that goes into a jar. This practice may seem easy at first, but, over time, you will need to think more creatively about what makes you feel grateful.

- **Laugh:** It might seem silly, but laughter can make difficult situations easier. Keep a joke book handy or plan a comedy movie night with friends. A game night can also be a great source of laughter.

- **Gratitude Affirmations:** For example, "I am so grateful for ..." or "Thankfulness, appreciation, and gratitude are part of who I am."

- **Help Others:** Kindness goes hand in hand with gratitude and positivity. Helping others makes you feel good, but also helps you recognize all the good things you have in your life.

- **Be Present:** Ground yourself in the present moment instead of worrying about what has happened or what could happen. Try this simple grounding exercise: What can you see around you? What can you hear and smell? How do your clothes feel on your body?

BUILDING MENTAL AND EMOTIONAL STRENGTH

The ability to be optimistic comes from mental and emotional strength. Unfortunately, your brain doesn't automatically default to positivity and resilience. You have to train it, and part of that is looking after yourself and your mental health.

Make Time to Relax:

- Stop scrolling and read a book instead.
- Get outside, preferably barefoot.
- Do something creative.
- Quiet your mind with a mindful activity, like doing a puzzle.

Mental and emotional strength require connection, confidence, and commitment. Invest time and energy into looking after yourself and your relationships. Make time for the people who fill your cup with positive vibes, and commit to being more present when you're with them. Try tech-free hangouts, weekend picnics, or craft sessions.

When you are mentally and emotionally strong, failure isn't so scary.

Turning a Setback into a Comeback

Failure brings new opportunities and a wealth of knowledge you can use. Failing helps you make informed decisions, so you don't repeat your mistakes. Failure isn't an ending, but a beginning.

Take the Post-It, for example. The simple, sticky pieces of paper you use when studying were created by mistake. A scientist was trying to make a stronger adhesive when he discovered that the weaker adhesive was reusable. What was a setback in the journey to find a strong glue led to the creation of a staple office item.

Failing Forward

The idea of "failing forward" comes from a book by John C. Maxwell. Failing forward means purposefully and deliberately using failure. Essentially, it's learning by doing.

When you fail forward, you don't label yourself a failure. Instead, you separate the failure from who you are as a person. When you look at failure objectively, you can see it as progress, moving you closer to your goal. Failure isn't final. *For example, 12 publishers rejected J.K. Rowling's Harry Potter manuscript, and we know how that turned out.*

Failing forward means owning your mistakes instead of blaming other people. When you see failure as negative, you can develop a victim mentality. A victim mentality is when you think life is happening to you and you have no control over it. But that's not true. You have the power to turn failure into fertilizer. Fertilizer? Yes, failure can be full of all the elements you need to thrive and grow, regardless of your situation.

How Can You Fail Forward?

Start small. Choose something you're afraid of and do it. Try out for the debate team or learn Latin. Anything that makes you nervous can be a starting point for failing forward.

For example, failing your driving test might upset and embarrass you. However, instead of viewing it as a failure, use it as an opportunity to identify areas for improvement that will make you a safer driver. You can practice specific maneuvers or techniques with a driving instructor or family member and review the rules of the road before trying again.

Facing Failure

Everyone fails — a lot! If you are not failing, you aren't trying. Failure means you were brave and took a chance. When failure comes knocking, invite it in, get to know it, and be friendly. Don't shut the door, because you never know what fantastic learning opportunity you might miss.

As John C. Maxwell once said, "Fail early, fail often, but always fail forward."

FRIENDS AND FAMILY

"There's always a little truth behind every 'Just kidding,'
a little knowledge behind every 'I don't know,' a little
emotion behind every 'I don't care,' and a little pain
behind every 'It's okay.'"
– Unknown

Did you know that healthy relationships based on connection and love can help you live longer? Research shows that people with strong social relationships have a 50% increased likelihood of survival (*Relationships Improve Your Odds of Survival by 50 Percent, Research Finds*, 2010). Why? Well, when you have healthy, happy relationships and feel connected to a community, you look after yourself better, take fewer risks, and manage stress better.

You may have noticed that your relationships have been shifting lately — and that's normal! You are changing and growing into yourself, which should change how you relate to those around you. You're probably spending more time with your friends, which may change your relationship with your parents.

Relationships are complex (even the easy ones) because people are unique. But complex doesn't have to mean complicated. Friendships and relationships take work, but they are vital. Life would certainly be dull without them. So, pull up your sleeves and get ready to work as we learn how to create and manage lasting relationships.

Making and Maintaining Meaningful Friendships

Time. Effort. Understanding. Empathy. Patience. Self-awareness.

These are just some of the things you need to make and maintain meaningful friendships. Think of friendships like baking a cake. You need a recipe to help you get the layered, sweet, satisfying result you want. But there are thousands of different kinds of cakes, and each has different ingredients. Although they are unique in their own way, leaving out ingredients will change the cake you get.

Each friendship is different and requires a different combination of "ingredients" to make it work. But, like most cake recipes, some core ingredients will help your friendship to "bake" and grow.

TIPS FOR INITIATING AND NURTURING FRIENDSHIPS

You may already have a group of friends at school, or perhaps you still need to find your people. Meeting new people can be daunting, and if the thought of starting a conversation with a stranger makes you break out in a sweat, you're not alone.

But there are ways to make meeting people easier:

- **Join a Club Based on Your Interests:** For example, join a movie club or horse-riding group, if that's your thing. If you love reading, consider starting a book club. If a group isn't available, be brave enough to start one.
- **Volunteer:** Not only is there a good chance that the other people at the animal shelter have the same interest in animals as you, but it also gives you easy conversation starters.
- **Self-Esteem Affirmations:** Saying an affirmation in front of the mirror can feel silly, but it is a powerful way to train your brain. Here are some affirmations you can try:
    - "I am worthy of meaningful connections and genuine friendships."
    - "I am confident in my ability to connect with others authentically and build lasting friendships."

- "I embrace my uniqueness and celebrate the qualities that make me a great friend."
- "I am open to new experiences and opportunities to meet people who share my interests and values."
- "I trust myself to navigate social situations easily and gracefully, forming meaningful connections along the way."

Challenge:

Talk to one new person every day for a week. This challenge is about having a conversation, not just saying a quick hello. Who knows—you might make a new friend! Even if you don't, you've practiced being uncomfortable, and that will make meeting new people get easier.

Have some general questions ready to help get the conversation started:

- Coffee or tea?
- Have you listened to any good podcasts lately?
- I just finished reading "___". Do you like to read?
- Do you have weekend plans?

Try to be subtle and open. You don't want to come on too strong and scare the person away. It's easy to ramble when you are nervous, but try to make space for them to respond to your questions. Most people like to talk about themselves, so you just need to listen to what they're saying and gently prompt them to keep going.

Don't let the conversation be a one-off. Friendships take time to develop, so you need to nurture friendly feelings in the early stages.

Showing Friends You Care

When trying to foster friendships, you have to make an effort.

Showing genuine interest in what is important to your friends fosters authenticity, trust, and support. For example, you might not care about the plot twist in your friend's novel or the fact that they reached a new level in a video game, but if those things are important to them, they should matter to you.

When you are interested in your friends' lives, they feel seen, valued, and accepted. Your interest creates a safe space for them to be themselves and demonstrates your desire to understand their experiences and feelings. Your effort creates trust, which is the cornerstone of any relationship. Trust will get you through the hard times, so it's worth cultivating.

The Importance of Shared Values and Interests

When people share the same beliefs and values, it is easier to find common interests. Common values also create a sense of belonging and connection, forming a jumping-off point for friendships.

Liking the same things and having shared values also impacts your communication. You will be more open to meaningful, respectful conversations when you have some common ground.

The easiest way to find people with shared interests and values is to try out group activities.

REMEMBER!

Meeting people can feel scary, but the other person probably feels just as nervous as you!

Understanding the Qualities of a Good Friend

Friendship is a two-way street. You can't expect your friends to stick around if you aren't doing your part to keep the relationship thriving. Three core ingredients in any friendship are trustworthiness, empathy, and reliability.

TRUST

Trust has to be earned, and it can be devastating when it's lost. It also develops slowly over time. You must be honest with your friends, and should expect honesty in return.

But what does that honesty look like? You can start by sharing your thoughts, feelings, and experiences and letting your friends do the same without judgment. Be your friends' biggest cheerleader and support them when they need it. Show up for them, be kind, and stand up for them even if they aren't in the room.

EMPATHY

Empathy is the ability to imagine yourself in someone else's shoes. When your friend talks with you, validate their emotions.

For example:

> *Friend: "I feel really anxious about the upcoming exam. I'm worried I won't do well."*
>
> *You: "I hear you. It's completely normal to feel anxious before a big test. You've been studying hard, so it makes sense that you feel this way."*

The goal is to offer support without trying to "fix" the problem. Your friend just needs you to be there and listen. You can also say, "Would you like my opinion, or do you just want me to listen?" Sometimes, just being present in the moment is all your friends need, and it lets them know they can trust you.

RELIABILITY

Reliability is about consistently showing up for your friends in both good and bad times. Friendships shouldn't be one-sided; they're about mutual support. **Do you honor your commitments? Do you make time for your friends? Do they know they can count on you to be there for them, no matter what?**

You prove you're reliable in the small moments — by returning a borrowed book, answering a text, or saying no to gossip.

SELF-REFLECTION EXERCISE

Being a good friend is more than just hanging out and having fun — it's about supporting each other and building trust and empathy.

Are you a good friend? Here is a practical exercise to help you assess your "friend skills."

Part 1: Assessing Your Friendship Qualities

Trustworthiness

- Do my friends trust me to keep their secrets?
- Am I reliable and consistent in my actions and commitments?
- Do I follow through on my promises to my friends?

Empathy

- Do I actively listen to my friends when they're talking to me?
- Am I able to understand and validate their feelings and experiences?
- Do I offer support and encouragement when they're going through tough times?

Reliability

- Am I there for my friends when they need me, both in good times and bad?
- Do I keep in touch with my friends and maintain our connections?
- Can they count on me to be consistent and dependable?

Part 2: Making Changes

Ask your friends what it is like being friends with you. Ask them if there are ways you can be a better friend. This can be hard — no one likes criticism — but if your friendships mean a lot to you, you'll work to improve them.

RECOGNIZING GOOD FRIENDS

Being a good friend is one thing, but recognizing good friends is another. It's important to know what real friendship looks like — and there are a few ways to spot it.

Observation and Reflection

Think about your interactions with your friends. Do they make you feel good? Are they supportive? Can you be yourself?

Active Listening

Do your friends really hear what you are saying, or are they just listening? Can they see the emotions underneath the words? Do they interrupt you or brush aside your feelings?

Reliability and Dependability

Can you count on your friends to be there when you need them? Do they keep their promises? Are they a consistent part of your life, both in good times and bad?

Showing Appreciation

If you have amazing friends, you should show them how much they mean to you. Stable and positive friendships are seriously underrated, and you should let your friends know that you appreciate and value them.

- **Express Gratitude:** Say thank you! Showing gratitude doesn't require big gestures or gifts.
- **Celebrate Their Qualities:** Highlight the qualities that make your friends special and unique. Let them know how much you value them, whether it's their sense of humor, kindness, or unwavering loyalty.
- **Be Supportive:** Show that you value their friendship by being there for them when they need you (and even when they don't).

Navigating Conflicts and Setting Healthy Boundaries

Conflict might be stressful, but it's normal! It can sometimes feel like a dead-end situation filled with big feelings. However, you can learn how to manage conflict with confidence, respect, and empathy. Friends fight sometimes — you just need to learn how to fight the right way.

SUPER STRATEGIES FOR CONFLICT AND COMMUNICATION

Conflict often occurs when communication fails. If you have clear, open, and direct lines of communication with your friends, it's much harder for conflict to take over.

So, what does clear communication look like?

Reflective Listening

Think of yourself as a sounding board and let your friend's words bounce back to you. This will let them know you are listening and help ensure you understand what they are saying and feeling.

> *For example:* "So, what I'm hearing is that you felt frustrated when I forgot our plans."

Asking Open-Ended Questions

Open-ended questions promote deeper understanding and conversation. These questions can't be answered with a simple "yes" or "no," and asking them encourages your friend to elaborate on their thoughts and feelings.

> *For example:* "Can you tell me more about how you feel about the upcoming project?"

Using "I" Statements

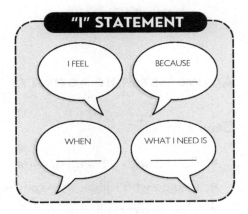

Using "I" statements when making requests or expressing your needs can help you sound less demanding or accusatory.

> *For example:* "I would appreciate it if you could let me know in advance if you're running late."

Seeking Clarification

Seek clarification if you're unsure about something the other person said or meant, as conflict often starts with miscommunication.

For example: "I'm not sure I understood your point. Could you please clarify?"

Active Problem-Solving

Try active problem-solving rather than blaming and criticizing each other. Conflicts don't resolve themselves!

For example: "Let's talk in turns and brainstorm ideas to address this issue."

ACTIVE LISTENING ACTIVITY

Step 1

- Pair up with a friend or family member.
- Decide who will be the "speaker" and the "listener" first.
- The speaker will share a personal story, experience, or feelings with the listener while the listener practices active listening.
- Afterward, switch roles, allowing both partners to experience being both speaker and listener.

Step 2

- Share your thoughts and feelings openly and honestly.
- Be specific about what you're sharing and how it makes you feel.

- Use "I" statements to express your thoughts and emotions ("I feel...," "I think...," "I noticed...").

Step 3

- Maintain eye contact and focus on the speaker without interrupting.
- Use nonverbal cues like nodding and facial expressions to show you're listening.
- Reflect back on what you hear by summarizing the speaker's main points and validating their feelings ("It sounds like you're feeling...," "It must have been difficult when...").

Step 4

- After each round of role-play, take a moment to reflect on the experience.
- Discuss what felt effective about the communication and what could be improved.
- Share insights on how active listening can enhance understanding and connection in relationships.

Conflict Resolution Questions

There are three core ingredients to navigating conflict: **understanding, compromise, and respect.**

Here are some quick questions to consider when de-escalating a conflict situation.

- Do you both want to sort the problem out and stop fighting?
- Can you identify the problem?
- Have you set ground rules for the conversation? For example, do not interrupt each other and keep things respectful.
- Are you both trying to be active, engaged listeners?
- What part of the conflict can you agree on?
- Is compromise an option?
- Can you agree to disagree?

Answering these questions can help you find a "peaceful" or "neutral" starting point. Also, if one of you doesn't want to resolve the conflict, then no amount of talking will help.

SETTING AND RESPECTING BOUNDARIES

Boundaries are important because:

- They are the limits you set to protect your emotional and physical health.
- They are an expression of self-worth, showing others that you respect yourself.
- They demonstrate to people how you want to be treated.
- They are crucial for healthy friendships and relationships.

- They ensure that all sexual encounters are consensual and comfortable for everyone involved.

Setting Boundaries

Setting boundaries can be difficult, but here are some tips to make the process easier.

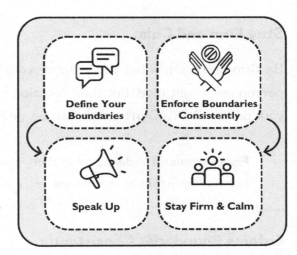

Clearly Define Your Boundaries

Use confident and respectful language to be direct and assertive when you enforce your boundaries. "I" statements are good here because they prioritize your needs and don't make others feel guilty or upset.

> **For example:** "I feel uncomfortable when you joke about my appearance. Please don't comment on my body."

Set Consequences

Boundaries only work when you consistently have consequences to back them up. You also need to communicate these consequences with your friends and family.

For example: "*If you keep commenting on my body, I will need to reconsider spending time together.*"

Stay Firm and Calm

Be firm and calm when you enforce your boundaries. The other person might get mad, but their reaction to your boundary is not your responsibility. Don't get defensive, and stay respectful.

For example: "*I understand you may disagree with my boundary, but it's important to me. I hope you can respect that.*"

Enforce Boundaries Consistently

Be consistent in enforcing your boundaries and following through on consequences if they are not respected. Consistency is key to reinforcing the importance of your boundaries and maintaining your self-respect.

For example, if a friend continues to pressure you to do something you're uncomfortable with, despite your boundaries, follow through on your consequences, such as limiting contact with them until they respect your boundaries.

Setting boundaries can be uncomfortable, and not everyone will agree with them, even when you communicate them clearly. But setting boundaries (and respecting other people's) is one of the most important things you can learn to do.

Be confident with your boundaries. People who don't respect boundaries often struggle with confrontation, so hold firm without being aggressive.

Understanding and Navigating Family Dynamics

Friendships can be tricky, especially when managing conflict. However, dealing with family relationships can be even more challenging.

Your relationship with your parents will change as you grow up. You may have already noticed some challenges in communicating and understanding each other.

- Sometimes, it feels like your parents don't understand where you're coming from, making it hard to talk to them.
- There may be power struggles as boundaries, rules, and expectations change.
- Screen time and social media can create friction and disconnect between you and your parents.

- You might find that you turn to your friends more than your parents. This can be hard for your parents, especially if they disagree with your choices.

It can be difficult, but try to see things from your parents' perspective. You are growing up in front of their eyes, and it can be hard for them to trust the process and give you the independence, autonomy, and respect you want.

Here are three strategies to help improve your relationship:

- **Strive for open, honest communication.** Talk with your parents (respectfully) and explain your point of view. Ask them to explain why they have specific rules or opinions so that you can see things from their perspective.
- **Ask your parents if you can set boundaries together.** For example, find curfew times you can agree on or work together to create boundaries around cell phone usage. Show your parents that they can trust you to be respectful and cooperative.
- **Show your parents that they can trust you.** Respect their boundaries and work on managing conflict situations without throwing a tantrum. If you want your parents to treat you differently, you must earn their trust.

As you grow up, you'll see your parents from a new perspective. You aren't a child anymore, and you'll start to see your parents as people, not just Mom and Dad. They have hopes, dreams, fears, and opinions, just like you. You aren't always going to see eye to eye, and that's okay. Just try to remember to show your parents the respect and empathy you want them to show you, because it's a two-way street.

Understanding and Respecting Family Values and Expectations

Does your family have certain values or traditions? Maybe your family values honesty and hard work. Perhaps you celebrate specific cultural holidays or always eat Sunday dinner at the table and have a family meeting.

Each family offers something unique in terms of values and traditions, and they are incredibly important. Your family is the first social group you belong to. They teach you about love, support, and societal norms. Family values and traditions shape your identity and help you figure out where you fit in.

Your parents have a huge influence on the person you become. Everything from discipline and expectations to advice and how they model respect and empathy influences who you become. But there are also intergenerational forces at play. Your family might have customs passed down from generation to generation based on your culture, religion, ethnicity, and nationality.

Your family values can have a positive or negative effect. They can make you feel confident and connected to something bigger than yourself, or they can encourage you to be closed-minded. The good news is that you can accept or reject your family values and traditions as you get older. This certainly isn't an either/or decision, but it is yours to make. Before you do, though, chat with your parents about your family history and ask them to explain why they think certain values or expectations are important.

Part of teen life is discovering who you are, both as an individual and as a family member.

The Importance of Friends and Family

Your support system includes both friends and family, which is crucial, especially during your teen years. Navigating the changing dynamics between you and your loved ones can be challenging, but it will all be okay.

Keep empathy and respect at the forefront of your mind when in a prickly situation, and remember that you don't have to go it alone.

5

EMOTIONS

"Feelings are much like waves, we can't stop them from coming, but we can choose which one to surf."
– Jonathan Martensson

Did you know that your teen brain is wired for emotional responses? So, if you have big feelings, don't panic! It's completely normal and is actually developmentally appropriate.

You might have heard people — maybe even your parents — talking about how moody and emotional you are. But did you know that neuroscience backs up the wild emotional ride teens experience? This means that what you're going through is completely normal.

The emotional part of your brain is called the limbic system, while the rational part is the prefrontal cortex. Your prefrontal cortex won't be fully developed until about age 25. During your teenage years, your limbic system is also underdeveloped and doesn't communicate with the prefrontal cortex as well as it should (Azab, 2020). On top of that, your limbic system is hyped up on hormones, making it hard to see things objectively. Essentially, your brain blows things out of proportion, making emotional regulation tricky.

What Is Emotional Regulation?

Emotional regulation is the ability to recognize, manage, and healthily respond to your emotions.

Emotional regulation involves:

- Being able to identify and label your emotions.
- Knowing what situations or thoughts trigger certain emotions.
- Accepting your feelings as they are, rather than trying to suppress or ignore them.
- Changing the way you think about a situation can change your emotional response.
- Understanding and respecting your emotional limits and setting boundaries.

Why Is Emotional Regulation Important?

The Importance of Self-Regulation

Helps Manage Stress
Stay calm and handle school stress better.

Builds Confidence
Feel better about yourself and bounce back from tough times.

Helps Clear Thinking
Stay calm to solve problems logically.

Improves Relationships
Talk calmly to reduce conflicts and strengthen friendships.

Emotional regulation is crucial because it affects so many parts of your life.

- Knowing how to handle your emotions helps you feel less anxious or down.
- Managing your emotions makes you less likely to feel overwhelmed or out of control.
- It helps you deal with school stress and anxiety more constructively.
- Talking about your feelings clearly and calmly can improve your relationships with friends, family, and teachers.

- Managing your emotions reduces the likelihood of snapping or getting into arguments.
- Staying calm helps you think through problems logically and find good solutions.
- It can boost your self-confidence and make you feel better about yourself.
- Emotional regulation helps you bounce back from tough times, making you more resilient.
- It helps you develop key social skills, like listening and resolving conflicts, which are essential for good relationships.

DID YOU KNOW? There's nothing wrong with being emotional. Your feelings are normal and can be big and overwhelming. There are no "bad" emotions, just inappropriate reactions. That's where emotional regulation comes in.

Recognizing and Naming Different Emotions

You can't validate your emotions if you don't know what you're feeling. The first step to becoming an emotional regulation pro is recognizing and naming your feelings.

IDENTIFYING AND ARTICULATING EMOTIONS

Do you remember the feelings wheel from Chapter 2? It is your best friend when figuring out what you're feeling. You can use a feelings wheel for both positive and negative emotions.

A feelings wheel usually has three rings. The innermost ring is for primary emotions, and the outer rings are for secondary emotions. Primary emotions like anger and happiness are the ones we often default to. But what if you aren't actually angry; what if you're frustrated or embarrassed, instead?

When identifying emotions, you also want to rate the emotion on a 1–10 intensity scale. How often do you feel this way? Do the same emotions pop up in similar situations? What does the emotion feel like in your body?

Answering these questions can sometimes be difficult, so try keeping an emotion diary. This will give you the opportunity to name your emotions, trace their origins, and understand the contexts in which they arise.

Emotion Diary

Week of: _____

EVENT What happened	BELIEF What you thought	EMOTIONS What you felt	BEHAVIOR What you did	OUTCOME
Friend didn't invite me to a party	He/She is mad and doesn't like me.	Rejected and mad	Will not talk to him/her	Our friendship is over.
Friend didn't invite me to a party	He/She might have her own private reasons & I respect that decision.	Calm, unbothered	Accept the decision and move on	Enjoy the next time you spend time and appreciate their presence.

Why Keep an Emotion Diary?

- **Self-Reflection:** Your Emotion Diary serves as a mirror. It lets you look back at situations and helps you identify your triggers and the big emotions that often pop up.

- **Emotion Regulation:** Identifying and naming your emotions is the first step toward mastering them. Your Emotion Diary helps you identify emotional patterns and work through your intense feelings.

- **Personal Growth:** Your teen years are about finding yourself and growing into your own person. An Emotion Diary helps you develop the self-awareness you need to become the person you want to be.

How to Use Your Emotion Diary

- **Daily Check-In:** Set aside a few minutes each day to check in with yourself. Notice any shifts in your mood throughout the day and jot down any situations or experiences that brought up strong feelings.
- **Name Your Emotions:** Practice accurately naming your emotions. Be honest about how you're feeling, even if it's uncomfortable.
- **Explore Contexts:** Dive deeper into the contexts surrounding your emotions. Ask yourself questions like, "What triggered this emotion?" "What thoughts or beliefs are underlying this feeling?" "How does this emotion manifest in my body?"
- **Track Patterns:** Review your Emotion Diary entries over time to identify patterns and trends in your emotional experiences. Are there recurring themes, triggers, and coping mechanisms?

You can also set a timer and just write. Give yourself the freedom to express yourself without a filter. Sometimes, you just need to get the feelings out of your head and heart and onto paper.

Here's an Example of Why Labeling Your Emotions Is Important

Researchers wanted to see if labeling emotions while facing fears could help people overcome them. They asked 88 people who were scared of spiders to get close to a live tarantula, and then divided them into four groups. Each group was given a list of words to describe their experience. The first group described their feelings about the spider using words like "anxious" and "frightened." The second group used neutral words to make the experience seem less scary. The third group said something unrelated to the spider, and the fourth group didn't say anything at all.

The participants were then exposed to the spider a second time. The researchers found that the first group, which accurately labeled their fear, did the best (Kircanski et al., 2012). They were able to get closer to the spider and were less scared than the other groups. This study showed the power of labeling emotions rather than ignoring or suppressing them.

Top Tip

When you name your emotions, you take your power back. Next time you're feeling overwhelmed, name what you are feeling and see if it helps.

UNDERSTANDING THE SPECTRUM OF HUMAN EMOTIONS

Humans are pretty special. We have the privilege of experiencing a wide range of emotions that add complexity to our experiences and interactions. Although some feelings aren't fun or easy to experience, they all serve a purpose.

Emotions are what you feel in response to things happening around you or inside your mind. They're complex reactions involving how you feel, physical changes in your body, how you think, and how you act. You might feel happy when you get a good grade, nervous before a big game, or sad when you fight with a friend. Many things can trigger your emotions, such as what's happening in your environment, thoughts, memories, or interactions with others.

Emotions Vary in Intensity and Frequency

Emotions can range from mild to really intense. For example:

- **Mild Emotion:** Feeling annoyed when you miss the bus.
- **Intense Emotion:** Feeling extreme fear if you're in a dangerous situation.

You can also experience emotions differently in terms of frequency:

- **Frequent Emotions:** Some feelings, like happiness or stress, might pop up almost daily.
- **Rare Emotions:** Others, like intense grief, might only occur in specific situations, such as losing a loved one or a special friendship.

Emotions Influence EVERYTHING!

Emotions are powerful because they affect how you think, act, and relate to your friends and family.

Thoughts: Your emotions can change the way you think. For instance:

- If you're feeling anxious, you might see things more negatively.

Actions: Emotions often drive you to act in certain ways, as well. For example:

- When you're happy, you might smile and laugh more.
- If you're angry, you might look for a fight or argue more.

Connections: Emotions help you connect with others.

- They help you experience empathy and put yourself in someone else's shoes.
- Emotions help you respond appropriately in social situations (don't worry if you still feel awkward, though).

Emotions don't always happen one at a time. Sometimes, they interact. One feeling can trigger another. For example, feeling embarrassed might make you feel angry at yourself. That's why emotional regulation is so important. You need to learn to handle everything your limbic system throws at you.

Becoming Emotionally Literate

What is emotional literacy, and why is it important?

Emotional literacy means you can recognize, name, and manage your emotions. It makes you "people-smart" because you can handle your emotions and behavior around others. It helps you develop strong relationships because you're in control of yourself.

Emotional intelligence isn't fixed. You can develop emotional literacy over time. A feelings wheel is a great first step, and an emotion diary is also helpful. You can also try a mood tracker, which gives you a snapshot of how you've been feeling over a period of time.

You have power over your mind and your moods. If you're always in a bad mood, you might be reacting to situations rather than responding to them. Reactions come from past experiences or stress about the future. **When you're grounded in the present moment, it's easier to respond with curiosity to the situation before you.**

Emotional Literacy Exercises

Pause and Breathe

It sounds simple, but stopping to breathe when you're feeling emotional can give you the space you need to respond rather than react.

- Take a deep breath through your nose for a count of four.
- Hold your breath for a count of four.
- Exhale slowly through your mouth for a count of four.
- Repeat this process until you feel more centered.

Do a Body Scan

When you feel emotionally out of control, a body scan can help ground you in the moment and create a space between reactivity and responsiveness.

Notice how your body feels. Are your fists clenched? Is your jaw tight? Are your shoulders up by your ears?

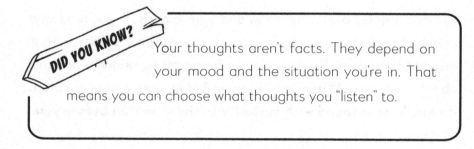

DID YOU KNOW? Your thoughts aren't facts. They depend on your mood and the situation you're in. That means you can choose what thoughts you "listen" to.

Identify and Challenge Negative Thoughts

Negative thoughts can trigger strong emotional reactions. Learning to identify and challenge these thoughts can help you respond more rationally.

- **Notice when you have a negative thought**, like "I'm going to fail this test."
- **Ask yourself if the thought is based on facts or assumptions.**
- **Challenge the thought.** For example, replace "I'm going to fail this test" with "I've studied hard, and I'll do my best. If I don't do well, I can learn from it."

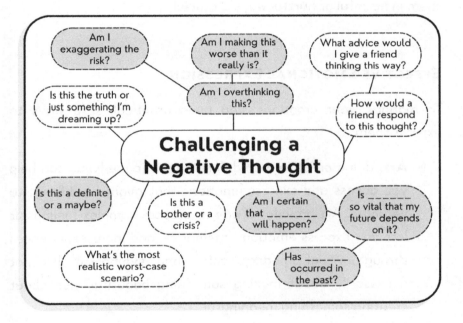

Healthy emotional regulation includes the ability to express and manage one's emotions in a healthy and productive way.

Healthy Ways to Express and Manage Emotions

All of your emotions are normal and healthy. They offer you unique experiences and help you learn and grow. Understanding how to validate and move through your feelings rather than reacting to them in harmful or hurtful ways is crucial.

EFFECTIVE EMOTIONAL EXPRESSION

To manage your emotions, you need practical, safe ways to express them.

- **Art:** Being creative with different artistic mediums can help you access and express emotions that might be difficult to verbalize. Art provides a way to process complex feelings. It lets you express emotions, memories, and inner experiences through visual imagery, color, and symbolism. It's not necessarily about making something beautiful — it's about creating something meaningful.

- **Music:** Have you ever felt emotional listening to a song? Or do you listen to specific playlists depending on your mood? Music is a highly effective way to express and process emotions. A systematic review of research into the effects of music on adolescent health found that music significantly impacts emotional expression and regulation (Chen, 2023).

- **Journaling:** Journaling is one of the most effective tools in your emotional regulation toolkit. Your journal provides a private, non-judgmental space to express your thoughts, feelings, and experiences. You can write freely about your emotions, concerns, and reflections in a stream-of-consciousness style or through structured prompts. Journaling helps you externalize and organize your thoughts, gaining clarity and insight into your experiences.

- **Constructive Conversation:** Trusted friends, family members, or a therapist can help you express your emotions and receive validation and support. Sharing experiences, perspectives, and insights with people you trust creates connections. It also fosters empathy and mutual understanding, helping you process emotions and grow in your relationships.

But what do you do in those moments when your feelings seem too big?

MANAGING OVERWHELMING EMOTIONS

Sometimes, your emotions can feel too big for you to handle. This is entirely normal! You're not a robot. You live in a world where you have instant access to information about the world, but you're not meant to be bombarded with that much "stuff."

When you keep a tight lid on your emotions, they will eventually explode. Think about trying to push a beach ball underwater. You may be able to do it for a while, but eventually, it will launch out of the water, sending you flying.

Don't hesitate to say "no" when things get too much. You don't owe anyone your peace. When you are in an overwhelming situation, look for PEACE:

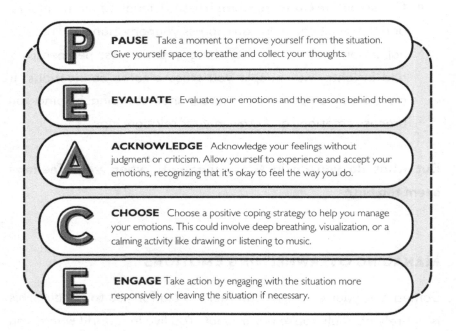

PAUSE Take a moment to remove yourself from the situation. Give yourself space to breathe and collect your thoughts.

EVALUATE Evaluate your emotions and the reasons behind them.

ACKNOWLEDGE Acknowledge your feelings without judgment or criticism. Allow yourself to experience and accept your emotions, recognizing that it's okay to feel the way you do.

CHOOSE Choose a positive coping strategy to help you manage your emotions. This could involve deep breathing, visualization, or a calming activity like drawing or listening to music.

ENGAGE Take action by engaging with the situation more responsively or leaving the situation if necessary.

Feelings become overwhelming when you don't practice "emotional maintenance." Developing healthy emotional habits is the best way to deal with overwhelming emotions.

Healthy Emotional Habits

Stay Active

- **Why:** Exercise isn't just good for your body — it's great for your mind, too! It releases endorphins, which are chemicals that make you feel happier.
- **How:** Find something you enjoy, like playing sports, dancing, biking, or even just going for a walk. Aim for at least 30 minutes of activity most days.

Get Enough Sleep

- **Why:** Sleep is super important for your mood and overall health. Without enough sleep, you can feel cranky, stressed, and overwhelmed.
- **How:** Try to get 8–10 hours of sleep each night. Create a bedtime routine that helps you relax, like reading a book or listening to calming music.

Eat Well

- **Why:** What you eat can affect how you feel, and being hangry (hungry + angry) is a real thing. Eating a balanced diet helps keep your energy up and your mood stable.
- **How:** Eat plenty of fruits, veggies, whole grains, and protein. Don't skip meals, and try to limit junk food and sugary drinks.

Practice Mindfulness

- **Why:** Mindfulness helps you stay grounded and aware of the present moment, making it easier to manage stress and emotions.
- **How:** Spend a few minutes each day practicing deep breathing or meditation. Use an app to guide you through mindfulness exercises.

Set Realistic Goals

- **Why:** Having goals gives you direction and purpose, but unrealistic goals can make you feel bad about yourself. Achieving realistic goals boosts your confidence and makes you feel good about yourself.
- **How:** Set small, achievable goals for yourself. Break bigger goals into smaller steps, and celebrate your progress.

Do Things You Enjoy

- **Why:** Taking time for hobbies and activities you love helps you relax and feel happy.
- **How:** List things you enjoy doing, like drawing, playing an instrument, or cooking. Schedule time each week to do at least one of these activities.

Going with the Emotional Flow

Emotions are a gift that you should embrace. They are the magic in the most important moments of your teen years. Good, bad, and everything in between, emotions create connections and deepen your interactions with the people around you.

Learning how to "feel your feelings" and consciously respond to them is an essential life skill.

When validating your feelings and moving through them, Dr. Seuss has it right: **"If things start happening, don't worry, don't stew, just go right along, and you'll start happening, too."**

HAPPINESS

"Now and then it's good to pause in our pursuit of happiness and just be happy."
– Guillaume Apollinaire

What makes you happy? Happiness isn't the same for everyone. It's like pizza toppings — what one person loves, another might hate. Spending time with friends might recharge you, but drain others. The key is to figure out what lights you up inside.

What Is Happiness?

Everyone experiences happiness in different ways. You may feel excited, relaxed, or joyful when you're happy.

Positive psychology researcher Sonja Lyubomirsky describes happiness as "the experience of joy, contentment, or positive well-being, combined with a sense that one's life is good, meaningful, and worthwhile" in her book *The How of Happiness*.

Happiness occurs when you are living a meaningful and authentic life.

Why Is Happiness Important?

Happiness is important because it is a state of being, not a destination. When you are happy, your life is filled with people and activities that bring joy, fulfillment, and satisfaction. Happiness is crucial for your mental and emotional well-being, helping you build stronger relationships, feel more confident, and handle stress more effectively.

Identifying Activities and Habits That Promote Happiness

Think about the things you love doing. Is it playing video games, reading, dancing, or maybe hiking? When you have free time, what do you fill it with? When you're daydreaming in math class, what are you thinking about doing?

Your hobbies, interests, and activities can bring pockets of joy into your life and contribute to a sense of balance. Sometimes, though, it can be tricky to identify what makes you really happy. Here are a few questions to get you thinking:

- What activities make you lose track of time?
- When do you feel the most relaxed?
- What do you look forward to doing on weekends or after school?

Exploring Personal Interests and Passions

Happiness comes from moments of joy and contentment, so you want to integrate as many of them into your days as possible. The things that make you happy might help you work toward a bigger goal.

DID YOU KNOW? Your teenage brain loves dopamine, a pleasure-based hormone that gets released when you do things you enjoy.

How to Add More Pleasure to Your Life and Increase Happiness

- **Set Aside Dedicated Time:** Work hobbies and activities into your week. Schedule them like homework or sports practices. Leisure time should be just as important as school and other commitments.
- **Combine Activities:** If you love spending time with your friends and enjoy being outside, have a picnic, go for a hike, or plan a barbecue.
- **Explore New Interests:** Don't be afraid to try new things. You'll never know what joy-bringing experience is around the corner if you don't put yourself out there.

Taking the time to do things you love can dramatically improve your life. Imagine if you only filled your days with school, homework, and responsibilities. There's not much balance there, right?

Three Vital Reasons for Prioritizing Hobbies (and Happiness)

1. **You'll Feel More Relaxed and Less Stressed:** Doing things you love can help you unwind and take your mind off school, friends, and your future.
2. **It Boosts Your Self-Esteem:** Achieving goals and improving your skills in areas you're passionate about can make you feel more confident.

3. **You'll Experience More Joy:** Hobbies and activities that light you up create "joy pockets" in your week.

Don't overthink it. Start with something small you can do every day, whether that's reading a chapter of a book before bed or listening to your favorite song while brushing your teeth. Joy shouldn't be a chore.

BENEFITS OF PHYSICAL ACTIVITY AND CREATIVE OUTLETS

Engaging in physical activities and creative pursuits isn't just about staying fit or productive — it's also a fantastic way to boost your mood and increase happiness. When you exercise, your body releases endorphins — those "feel-good" chemicals that can make you feel happier and more relaxed.

Being creative is a seriously underrated happiness flex. When you're engaged in a creative activity, like gardening or building Lego, you're grounded in the present moment, helping you feel more joyful and content.

Finding Balance

Life isn't just one happy ride. In fact, how would you recognize happiness if you hadn't experienced pain, disappointment, and sadness?

The key is finding a balance between your responsibilities and the things that bring you joy — and better yet, finding ways to make the "boring" stuff more joyful.

First, don't feel guilty about taking time for yourself. These activities aren't just fun — they're essential for your mental and emotional health. For example, if you're busy with schoolwork, take short breaks to do something you love. Even 10 minutes can make a big difference.

Second, set boundaries and don't overcommit. It's easy to get overwhelmed if you try to do too much. Be realistic about what you can handle and set aside time for rest and relaxation. It's okay to say no sometimes.

Making time for things that bring you joy and fulfillment isn't just about having fun. It's also about building a rich and satisfying life. When you do what you love, you're not only happier, but you also handle stress better and feel more confident.

REMEMBER!

It's not selfish to prioritize things that make you happy.

The Role of Gratitude and Positive Thinking

You may find it hard to find joy when life, friendships, and school feel overwhelming. That's where gratitude comes in. What if you reframed your responsibilities?

Instead of saying, "I have to..." try saying, "I get to..."

It seems like a small change, but the impact can be profound. Gratitude has a sneaky way of doing that.

What Is Gratitude?

Gratitude is feeling thankful for what you have rather than upset over what you don't have. It's a perspective shift that makes your life more abundant.

Here's an example: Imagine you didn't get the latest smartphone like some of your friends did. Instead of feeling upset or jealous, try focusing on what you do have. Maybe your current phone still works fine and allows you to stay in touch with your friends, listen to music, and take photos. By feeling grateful for what your phone can do, rather than focusing on what it can't, you shift your perspective and start appreciating what you already have.

Why Is Gratitude Important?

Gratitude helps you notice the small things in your life that can bring you joy. It gives you an appreciation for the life you have, rather than living in the past or present, wishing for the things you don't have.

Gratitude has a snowball effect. The more things you feel grateful for, the happier you are. When you have a grateful mindset, you spread positivity and joy, making you feel good.

CULTIVATING GRATITUDE

Cultivating gratitude is a simple but powerful way to boost your mood and sneak more happiness into your life.

Here are some simple gratitude hacks you can try:

- **Gratitude Journal:** Keep a journal where you write down three things you're thankful for every day. They don't have to be huge. Write down anything that made you happy or grateful that day.
- **Say Thanks:** Make it a habit to say thank you to people who make your day better. It could be your parents, friends, teachers, or even the bus driver.
- **Gratitude Letters:** Write a letter to someone who has made a positive impact on your life. You don't even have to send it. Just writing it can make you feel good.

When you focus on what you're grateful for, you start to notice more good things in your life. It's like switching on a light in a dark room — you suddenly see things you didn't notice before. Gratitude helps you shift your focus from what's missing to what's already there.

DID YOU KNOW? Gratitude helps your brain release dopamine and serotonin. These neurotransmitters improve your mood and help you feel happy (Ba, 2024).

THE POWER OF POSITIVE THINKING AND REFRAMING CHALLENGES

Jim Rohn once said, "Happiness is not by chance but by choice." The same goes for positivity.

What Is Positive Thinking?

Positive thinking is about focusing on the good things in your life and keeping a hopeful attitude, even when things get tough. It doesn't mean ignoring your problems or pretending everything is perfect. Instead, it's about looking for solutions, staying hopeful, and seeing the bright side of situations.

> *For example, if you did poorly on an exam, you can recognize that, while it's disappointing, you can learn from the experience and try harder next time. It's about believing that you can improve and things can get better.*

Why Is Positive Thinking Important?

Positive thinking makes your life better. That may sound cheesy, but it's true.

- **A positive attitude makes you easier to be around.**
- **Positive thinking helps you stay focused and achieve your goals.**

- **A positive mindset helps you make healthier lifestyle choices.**
- **Focusing on the positive reduces stress and helps you feel more relaxed and happy.**

One of the most important ways positivity improves your life is by helping you look for opportunities rather than problems. Positivity also helps you be kinder to yourself and those around you. With a positive attitude, the world opens up and seems alive with possibilities.

ADOPTING AN OPTIMISTIC MINDSET

So, what does a positive mindset look like, and how can you train your brain to see the good instead of the bad?

The "Glass Half Full vs. Half Empty" Concept

You've probably heard the saying, "Is the glass half full or half empty?" It's a simple way to explain how people view the world. Someone who sees the glass as half full focuses on the positive side — they're optimistic. On the other hand, someone who sees the glass as half empty focuses on the negatives — they're pessimistic.

Think about two people you know. One of them might always find something good in every situation, even when things go wrong.

That's the "glass half full" person. The other might often complain or see the downside, even when things are going well (everyone has that one friend who can be a bit of a downer). That's the "glass half empty" person. Now, ask yourself: Which one would you rather hang out with?

Switching to a more positive mindset can be challenging. Here are some simple and effective strategies to help you be a "glass half full" person:

- **Challenge Negative Thoughts:** When you notice yourself thinking negatively, hit pause and consider if there's a different way to view the situation. For instance, instead of thinking, "I'll never get this math problem," try saying, "This is tricky, but I can figure it out with some help and practice."
- **Focus on Solutions, not Problems:** Instead of getting stuck on what's wrong, focus on what you can do to improve things. If you're struggling with a project, think about steps you can take to improve, like asking for help or breaking the project into smaller, more manageable parts.
- **Surround Yourself with Positive Influences:** Hang out with people who lift you up and support you. Positive friends and family can help you see the good in situations and encourage you when you are feeling down.
- **Recognize and Celebrate the Good in Everyday Life:** Make it a habit to notice and appreciate the little things that make

you happy. It could be a kind word from a friend, a tasty snack, or a beautiful sunset. Take a moment each day to reflect on these good moments.

Recognizing and celebrating the little wins in everyday life is super important. It helps you get into the habit of thinking positively, which can really boost your mood and overall outlook on life.

By thinking optimistically, you can improve your mental health, build stronger friendships, and feel more motivated and confident when facing challenges. Remember, it's not about ignoring the bad stuff, but about finding the good and working towards making things better.

Happiness Is a Work in Progress

Happiness is a journey, not a destination. It's a work in progress that involves making a series of choices every day. **It's about choosing to stay positive, having a realistic attitude, and being persistent, even when things get tough.** Happiness doesn't happen overnight. It takes effort and a mindset that focuses on the good. Remember, it's okay to have off days, but by consistently choosing positivity and working towards what makes you happy, you'll build a more fulfilling and joyful life.

STUDIES

"The secret of success is to do the common things uncommonly well."
– John D. Rockefeller

Are studies getting you down?

At this stage in life, studies may be taking up a lot of your mental space. You're probably thinking about college and what you want your life to look like after you graduate. These are big questions that can be overwhelming and a bit scary.

There are many things you can't control about your future, but studying isn't one of them. You can learn how to learn. More importantly, you can learn how to learn in a way that works for you.

As Rockefeller said, **"The secret of success is to do the common things uncommonly well."** You don't have to be the best student to learn how to study effectively. Taking notes, making summaries, and managing your time are crucial skills that can put you ahead of the pack.

Effective Study Habits

Studying is a skill you can develop. The trick is finding the best strategies for your brain and setting yourself up for success with a learning space you enjoy. **You don't have to love studying to be good at it.**

Creating a Conducive Study Environment

Your study space is critical to learning success. It should be distraction-free, organized, and equipped with everything you need for a study session. While it may be tempting to study on your bed, it's better to have a designated study area where you can focus and signal to your brain that it's time to work.

Personalize your study space to make it inviting and motivational. Consider adding:

- Motivational posters and quotes
- Goal trackers and vision boards
- Plants

- Bulletin boards or calendars
- Colored pens and sticky notes
- Snacks and fidget toys

An organized, personalized, distraction-free space will help you focus and be more productive.

DID YOU KNOW?

Around the world, students without a desk are three times more likely to be at the bottom academically than at the top. (Rutkowski & Hastedt, n.d.)

Techniques for Effective Note-Taking, Revision, and Exam Preparation

Exams are more than tests at the end of the semester — they are a culmination of small daily actions that you have the power to excel at.

Note-Taking Techniques

Taking notes during class is one way to make studying easier.

OUTLINE METHOD

This structured approach allows you to create a map of the lesson with main topics and subtopics. It's perfect for content-heavy subjects.

Reasons to Love It:

- There is an information hierarchy.
- You can group information.
- The notes are easy to read and follow.

Social Media and Its Impact on Teens

A. Overview of Social Media Usage

I. Stats

1.1 Over 90% of teens use social media on a regular basis.

1.2 Most popular platforms include TikTok, Instagram and Snapchat.

B. Positive and Negative Impacts

I. Positive Impacts

1.1 Connection: Helps people stay connected, build friendships.

1.2 Expression: Promotes creativity, sharing interests and stories

2. Negative Impacts

12.1 Mental Health: Increased anxiety, depression and FOMO.

2.2 Bullying: Increased incidents of cyberbullying and online harassment.

How It Works:

1. Begin your notes with the main topics or headings. These are the big ideas or critical points your teacher is talking about. Write these main topics at the far left of your page.
2. Under each main topic, add subtopics or key points that relate to it. Indent these subtopics slightly to the right.
3. Under each subtopic, add specific details, examples, and explanations. Indent these even further to the right.
4. Use bullet points or numbers to make your notes easy to read. This helps you quickly find and review information later.

CORNELL METHOD

This method helps you get actively involved in the process, which can help the information stick.

Reasons to Love It:

- Helps you keep your notes clear and easy to review.
- Writing cues and summaries reinforce your understanding.
- Makes revising for exams quicker.

Note taking	Name, Date, Subject, Topic
Cue Column	**Note Taking Column**
Complete this after class. Include keywords, questions, or main ideas. Use it to help you quickly recall important points when reviewing your notes later. It's also helpful for self-testing.	This is where you take your main notes during class or while studying. You might want to include: • Main points, details and examples • Diagrams, graphs, drawings or charts • Bullet points • Short hand symbols / paraphrases / abbreviations
WHAT'S, WHO, WHEN'S and WHERE'S	You might say this column is for the WHY'S and HOW'S

Summary Section

After your notes are complete, write a brief summary of the main points covered. This summary should be a few sentences that summarise the material. It helps reinforce what you've learned and provides a quick reference when reviewing.

How It Works:

1. Draw a vertical line about 2.5 inches from the left edge of your page. This creates two columns: a narrow left column for cues and a wider right column for notes.

2. Leave a few inches at the bottom of the page for the summary section.

3. Write down key points, details, and main ideas during class in the right-hand column. Write in short, concise phrases without worrying about complete sentences.

4. After class, review your notes and use the left-hand column to write cues. These are questions, keywords, or main concepts related to the notes you took.
5. Write a brief summary of the notes at the bottom of the page. This will help reinforce what you've learned and provide a quick review for future studying.

BOXING METHOD

The Boxing Note-Taking Method is a modern approach designed to help you visually organize information into boxes for each topic.

Reasons to Love It:

- It's a very visual method.
- Very helpful for revision.
- Helpful for focusing on one topic at a time.

How It Works:

1. Start by drawing boxes on your note page. Each box will contain notes on a single topic or concept. Leave some space between the boxes to visually separate the topics.
2. Write the title or main idea of each topic at the top of each box. This will help you quickly identify what each box contains.

Advantages

- Keeps notes organized and neat & makes it easy to group info together
- Looks great, especially if you design it like a bullet journal

Limitations

- Difficult to use in live lectures or classes as it takes time to organize
- Not great for subjects with lots of detailed content

Best Use For

- Revision notes and cheat sheets
- Subjects where you can break topics into smaller sections
- Subjects with a mix of things like definitions, formulas, and diagrams, which can be listed as bullet points.

How to Use the Boxing Method

SUBTOPIC

The information within these boxes can come in any form

SUBTOPIC

SUBTOPIC

SUBTOPIC

SUBTOPIC

3. During class or while reading, jot down key points, definitions, diagrams, or other relevant information within the appropriate boxes.

4. Use bullet points, numbers, or short phrases to keep your notes concise and organized.

5. Use different colors for headings, important points, or highlights. This adds an extra layer of organization and makes your notes more interesting.

MIND MAP METHOD

A free-flowing and creative method, mind mapping involves creating diagrams that connect related concepts and information, making it easier to see the big picture and understand how different pieces of information are related.

Reasons to Love It:

- Allows you to link topics and make connections.
- Lets you get creative, even with non-creative topics.
- Can be used for brainstorming, planning, and studying a wide range of topics.

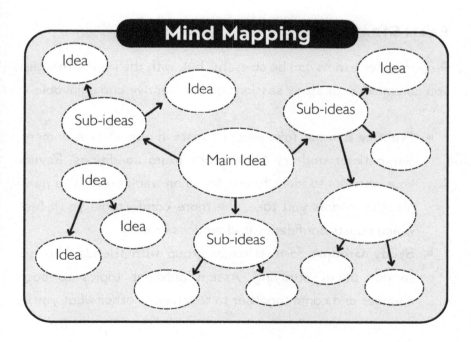

How It Works:

1. Write the main topic or idea in the center of your page. This is your starting point.
2. From the central idea, draw branches outward for each subtopic or main point. Label each branch with a subtopic.
3. From each subtopic, draw smaller branches to add details, examples, or related ideas. Continue branching out as needed.
4. Use different colors for different branches. Adding images, symbols, or doodles can also help you remember information better.
5. Use keywords or short phrases rather than full sentences to keep your mind map clear and concise.

EXAM STRATEGIES

Preparing for exams can be stressful, but, with the right strategies, you can make your study sessions more effective and enjoyable.

- **Practice Exams:** Take practice tests in a quiet environment. Set a timer and try to recreate exam conditions. Review your answers to identify and focus on weak areas. The more practice exams you take, the more comfortable you'll feel, which boosts confidence and reduces anxiety.
- **Study Groups:** Form a study group with friends who are serious about studying. Assign different topics to each member and come together to teach each other what you've

learned. Keep sessions organized with an agenda to avoid wasting time.

- **Active Recall Methods:** Use flashcards, teach what you've learned to someone else, and self-quiz to actively engage with the material.

Combining practice exams, study groups, and active recall methods can supercharge your exam preparation.

- **Plan Ahead:** Create a study schedule that includes time for making notes and group study sessions. Work backward from your exam date to ensure you have enough time to cover everything without cramming.
- **Mix It Up:** Don't rely on just one study method. Mixing different techniques can help keep things interesting and enhance your understanding.
- **Take Breaks:** Schedule regular breaks to avoid burnout. Short breaks can help you stay focused and retain information better.

Strategies for Managing Time Effectively and Avoiding Procrastination

All these study techniques are useless if you don't have a realistic study schedule that you can stick to.

Tips for Managing Your Time

Allocate Time Wisely
Spend more time on challenging or important topics.

Chunking
Divide large topics into smaller, manageable chunks.

Set Small Goals
Establish achievable study goals for each session.

Daily Study Plan
Allocate specific times each day for studying. Consistency is key.

Balance
Balance study time with fun.

Include Breaks
Schedule short breaks between study sessions to maintain focus.

Overcoming Procrastination

Procrastination can sneak up on anyone, but you can tackle it head-on with a few fun and creative strategies.

- **Gamify Your Tasks:** Turn your study sessions into a game. Award yourself points for completing tasks, or challenge your friends to a study contest, like who can get the highest score on a practice quiz. Friendly competition is a great motivator.
- **The Pomodoro Technique with a Twist:** The Pomodoro Technique is a classic studying technique, but you can make

it more fun with dance breaks or snack rewards. For example, take a 5-minute dance break after every 25-minute study session, or have a healthy snack after each study session.

- **Study in a New Location:** Sometimes, a change of scenery can boost your productivity. Find a cozy café or a quiet spot in the library, or take your study materials outdoors if the weather is nice.
- **Study Buddy System:** Pair up with a friend to keep each other accountable. Schedule regular study sessions with a friend. Share your goals and check in regularly to stay on track.

Don't overcomplicate studying. Try strategies to bust procrastination, create a study-friendly environment, and establish a study schedule.

Coping with Academic Pressure and Stress

Academic pressure and stress are normal. You want to do well and make yourself and your parents proud. However, juggling friends, relationships, and extracurricular activities can be challenging, leading to stress spilling into all areas of your life.

TECHNIQUES FOR STRESS REDUCTION

School can be stressful, especially when exams and deadlines pile up. But don't worry, there are some simple ways to manage that stress.

- **Short Breaks:** During long study sessions, take short breaks to do deep breathing or take a quick walk. It can help you return to your work feeling refreshed and focused.
- **Hobby Time:** Schedule time for hobbies like drawing or a quick workout. Balancing work with play is key to managing stress.
- **Laughter Therapy:** They say laughter is the best medicine, and it's true! Watch a funny movie, check out hilarious YouTube videos, or scroll through memes that make you laugh.
- **Nature Time:** Take a walk in the park, go for a hike, or just sit in your backyard.
- **Video Game Breaks:** Playing video games (in moderation) can be a great way to de-stress. Choose fun and not too intense games that make you feel good without adding more stress.
- **Mindful Coloring:** Use a coloring book and pencils to calm your mind.
- **Practice Mindfulness:** Try a guided meditation app, do some breathing exercises, or simply sit quietly and focus on your surroundings for a few minutes.

DID YOU KNOW? To help with stress, Bill Gates reads for an hour before bed, and Warren Buffet plays the ukulele (Dodgson, 2017).

IMPORTANCE OF A BALANCED LIFESTYLE

Many adults struggle with a balanced lifestyle, so don't worry if you haven't figured it out yet. Finding balance is harder than it looks. Balance is the idea that you can experience happiness and fulfillment in some areas of your life without negatively impacting other areas.

Finding balance is like finding a unicorn. However, some things can make balance easier.

Adequate Sleep

Sleep is essential for your body and mind to function properly. Getting enough rest helps you:

- **Improve Memory and Concentration:** Sleep enhances your ability to focus and retain information, which is crucial when studying.
- **Boost Mood:** A good night's sleep can improve your mood.
- **Maintain Physical Health:** Sleep supports your immune system.

Proper Nutrition

What you eat has a direct impact on how you feel. Proper nutrition helps you:

- **Fuel Your Brain:** Nutrient-rich foods like fruits, vegetables, whole grains, and lean proteins provide the energy and nutrients your brain needs to function at its best.
- **Stabilize Energy Levels:** Eating balanced meals and healthy snacks throughout the day helps maintain steady energy levels.
- **Enhance Mood:** Certain foods, like those rich in omega-3 fatty acids, can boost your mood and reduce anxiety.

Leisure Activities

Taking time to do things you enjoy is just as important as studying. Leisure activities help you:

- **Reduce Stress:** Doing something fun can help lower your stress levels.
- **Boost Creativity:** Engaging in creative hobbies can spark your creativity and give you a mental break from school stress.
- **Build Social Connections:** Spending time with friends and family strengthens your support network, making coping with stress and challenges easier.

3 Ways to Find a Healthy Balance

1. Create a Realistic Schedule

- **Plan Ahead:** Use a planner or app to schedule your study time, activities, and rest.
- **Prioritize Tasks:** Identify the most important tasks and tackle them first. Break larger projects into smaller, manageable steps.

2. Set Boundaries

- **Limit Screen Time:** Too much time on devices can interfere with sleep and concentration. Set limits to ensure you have time for other things.
- **Say No When Necessary:** "No" is a complete sentence. It's okay to decline invitations or extra responsibilities if you need time to rest or focus.

3. Reflect and Adjust

- **Regular Check-Ins:** Take time to reflect on your schedule and lifestyle. Are you getting enough sleep? Are you feeling overwhelmed? Adjust your routines as needed.
- **Celebrate Achievements:** Recognize and celebrate your successes. This boosts your motivation and reinforces positive habits.

CULTIVATING A HEALTHY PERSPECTIVE ON ACADEMIC ACHIEVEMENT

Achieving academic success is important, but having a healthy perspective on what that success means is equally crucial.

Miriam-Webster defines "success" as a "favorable or desired outcome" ("Success," 2024). You get to decide on the desired outcome, though. Maybe it's getting a B in math or performing an hour of community service each week. You are the only person who gets to decide what your success looks like.

When it comes to academic success, a few things can keep you on track.

Setting Realistic Academic Goals

Setting goals is critical to staying motivated and focused. However, these goals must be realistic and attainable for you.

- **Be Specific:** Instead of setting vague goals, like "do better in math," set specific targets like "improve my math grade by one grade."
- **Break It Down:** Break your goals into manageable chunks. For example, if you need to write a history essay, set small goals, like researching, creating an outline, writing a draft, and making edits.

- **Set Timeframes:** Assign deadlines to help you stay focused and measure your progress.
- **Stay Flexible:** Adjust your goals as needed. If you find something isn't working, reevaluate and change your plan.

Recognizing Efforts and Progress

Often, we focus too much on the outcome, like grades or test scores, and forget to acknowledge the hard work and progress we've made along the way.

- **Celebrate Small Wins:** Acknowledge every step you take towards your goal. Did you finish your homework on time? Did you understand a tricky concept in class? Celebrate these small victories.
- **Reflect on Progress:** Keep a journal to note your progress and improvements.
- **Be Kind to Yourself:** Not every effort will lead to immediate success. Sometimes, you'll fail — and that's okay. Learn from these experiences and keep going.

Valuing Learning and Personal Growth

Grades are just one measure of academic success, but true learning and personal growth are far more valuable.

- **Learning Over Grades:** Have a goal of understanding and appreciating what you're learning rather than just aiming for a high grade. Good grades will follow when you truly understand the material.

- **Growth Mindset:** Adopt a growth mindset, focusing on improvement through effort. Instead of thinking, "I'm bad at math," try, "I'm working on improving my math skills."

- **Intrinsic Motivation:** Find your reasons for learning and succeeding. Your studies will be more meaningful when you're motivated by personal interest and the desire to grow, rather than just by external rewards like grades.

Studying Is a Skill You Can Cultivate

Learning is a lifelong adventure. Every challenge you face and every success you achieve is a stepping stone toward becoming the best version of yourself. But that doesn't mean you can't get serious about learning how to study, manage stress, and prioritize your time.

You have more control over your life and success than you may realize. That might seem daunting, but it shouldn't be. Knowing that you control a lot of your future is empowering, so embrace it.

HEALTH AND PERSONAL HYGIENE

"Take care of your body. It's the only place you have to live."
— Jim Rohn

Did you know your cell phone carries 10 times more bacteria than most toilet seats (Young, 2020)? Or that it takes only seven seconds for someone to form a first impression of you (First Impressions, 2024)?

What Is Health and Personal Hygiene?

Health is more than just not being sick — it's about feeling great physically, mentally, and emotionally. Personal hygiene involves keeping yourself clean and well-groomed, including showering regularly, brushing your teeth, washing your hands, and wearing clean clothes.

Health and personal hygiene go hand-in-hand and are both vital components of your successful transition to adulthood.

Daily Routines for Personal Cleanliness

REGULAR PERSONAL CARE ROUTINES

Do your parents still have to remind you about brushing your hair or teeth? That might have been okay when you were a little kid, but your teen body is a different beast. Learning how to look after it will dramatically change your life. Bathing, skincare, oral hygiene, and grooming aren't just about looking good — they're about feeling good, too. Taking care of yourself can boost both your physical and mental health. It's about prioritizing yourself, and it's an invaluable lesson to learn.

Bathing: More Than Just a Clean Slate

Jumping in the shower might seem like just another daily chore, but it's actually a chance to refresh your body and mind. A good shower can be like hitting the reset button, giving you a fresh start to kick off your day or unwind before bed.

Skincare: Love the Skin You're In

Your skin does a lot for you, from protecting your insides to helping you look your best. Show it some love with a simple routine, like a gentle cleanser to wash away dirt, a moisturizer to keep your skin hydrated, and sunscreen to protect you from harmful UV rays. Hormones can cause pimples, but a good skincare routine helps keep your skin clear.

Oral Hygiene: Your Smile's Best Friend

Brushing and flossing might seem like no-brainers, but they're crucial for maintaining a healthy smile. Regular brushing keeps your teeth clean and your breath fresh, making you feel more confident. Good oral hygiene habits now can save you from painful and expensive dental treatment down the road.

Grooming: The Finishing Touch

Grooming and hygiene aren't quite the same thing. You can be clean but not well-groomed. Grooming includes combing your hair, trimming your nails, and shaving. Presenting yourself well can give you that extra confidence boost. Plus, it's a form of self-respect. Taking the time to present yourself well shows that you value yourself.

Why It All Matters

Taking care of your body isn't just about avoiding your parents' nagging — it's about building a foundation for a healthier, happier you. When you prioritize personal care, you're telling yourself that you matter.

Practical Tips for Busy Teens

Finding time for self-care can be challenging, between school, sports, friends, and hobbies. Here are some tips to help you stay on top of your game.

- **Create a Routine:** Make personal care part of your daily schedule.
- **Keep It Simple:** A quick shower, basic skincare, and a few minutes for grooming can make a big difference.
- **Combine Tasks:** Listen to music or a podcast while you get ready.
- **Use Versatile Products:** Look for products that save time, like a two-in-one shampoo and conditioner or a moisturizer with SPF.

Taking care of yourself is more than just a daily task. It's a way to invest in your health and happiness and develop A+ habits. When you feel good inside and out, you're more confident, resilient, and ready to face whatever comes your way.

BENEFITS OF GOOD HYGIENE FOR HEALTH

Hygiene isn't just about your appearance. It's also about keeping your body healthy and germ-free. One study found that students touch their faces 23 times per hour (P, 2020). Imagine all the germs moving from your hands to your face if you aren't diligent about hygiene. Good hygiene is your first line of defense against germs and illnesses.

Understanding the Importance of Self-Care for Health and Well-Being

Taking care of your health isn't just about your body — it's also about your mind. When you feel rested, happy, and good about yourself, making healthy choices becomes a lot easier.

INCORPORATING SELF-CARE INTO DAILY ROUTINES

Self-care isn't just about treating yourself — it's about creating habits that keep you feeling good, inside and out. Here are some simple self-care hacks to help you fit it into your day:

- **Make It a Habit:** Self-care should be a regular part of your day, like brushing your teeth or doing homework. Start small and build up. Try a 10-minute walk after school or some lunges on your way to the bathroom.

- **Schedule It In:** Set specific times in your day for self-care. Put it in your calendar. Make these moments as important as any other activity.
- **Mix It Up:** Self-care doesn't have to look the same every day. One day, you might go for a run, and the next, you might draw or listen to music.
- **Listen to Your Body:** Pay attention to how you're feeling. If you're tired, make rest a priority. If you're stressed, take a break and do something relaxing.

What Does Self-Care Look Like?

Self-care is personal, so it'll look different for everyone. Here are some examples to get you started:

- **Regular Exercise:** It doesn't have to be intense, but even a short daily workout can make a big difference.
- **Mindful Eating:** Pay attention to what you eat and how it makes you feel. Notice the flavor, texture, and even the smell.
- **Relaxation Techniques:** This could be deep breathing exercises, meditation, yoga, or even taking a long bath. Find what helps you unwind and make it a regular practice.

Fun Self-Care Hacks

- **The 10-Minute Rule:** Struggling to start a new self-care habit? Commit to just 10 minutes. You'll often find that you'll want to keep going once you start.

- **Self-Care Jar:** Write different self-care activities on slips of paper and put them in a jar. Each day, pick one at random. This adds an element of surprise and keeps things fun.
- **Buddy System:** Find a friend to join you in your self-care activities. Having a buddy can make it more fun and keep you accountable. Run together, share healthy recipes, or do relaxation exercises.

Role of Nutrition, Exercise, and Sleep in Overall Health

Your body is a system. When one part is out of balance, it affects the others. During your teen years, when so much physical and mental growth is happening, your body needs sleep, nutritious food, and exercise.

EVERYTHING IS LINKED

- **Sleep:** When you sleep, your body is in repair mode. It gives your muscles time to recover and your brain time to process everything you learned during the day. Lack of sleep can affect your mood, focus, and overall performance. Have you noticed how much harder homework is when you're tired or how snappy you are with your friends and parents after a few late nights? Sleep is also when your body boosts your immune system, supports growth, regulates hormones, and keeps you healthy.

- **Nutrition:** The food you eat is your body's fuel. Nutritious food gives you the energy to do everything from paying attention in class to playing sports. Certain nutrients, like omega-3 fatty acids found in fish, help with memory and learning. Eating well also helps you sleep better, as foods rich in magnesium (like nuts and leafy greens) can help you relax and get a good night's sleep.
- **Exercise:** Being active during the day makes it easier to fall asleep at night and improves your sleep quality. Regular physical activity also supports both your mental and physical health, boosting mood and energy levels.

TIPS FOR CREATING A BALANCED ROUTINE: SLEEP, NUTRITION, AND EXERCISE

Sleep

- **Create a Sleep-Friendly Environment:**
  - **Fairy Lights and Comfy Blankets:** Make your bed inviting with soft blankets and twinkly lights.
  - **Cool and Comfortable:** Ensure your bedroom is cool, quiet, and dark. Use blackout curtains, a fan, or a white noise machine to block out distractions.

- **Limit Electronics:** Set a "no screens" rule in your bedroom and put devices away at least an hour before bed. Instead, listen to calming music or read a book.
- **Establish a Sleep Routine:**
  - **Consistency Is Key:** Go to bed and wake up at the same time every day, even on weekends, to regulate your body's internal clock.
  - **Wind-Down Time:** Start winding down an hour before bed. Use this time to relax and prepare for sleep.
  - **Relaxing Activities:** Engage in relaxing activities like reading, listening to calming music, or practicing deep breathing exercises. Avoid stimulating activities like video games or intense exercise right before bed.
  - **Track Your Sleep:** Use a sleep app or a journal to track your sleep patterns, and aim for 8–10 hours a night.

Sleep Tracker

Week of: _____

	TIME TO SLEEP	TIME AWAKE	HOURS OF SLEEP	SLEEP NOTES
Monday				
Tuesday				
Wednesday				
Thursday				
Friday				
Saturday				
Sunday				

- **No Caffeine:** Avoid coffee and late-night snacks close to bedtime. They can keep you awake and make it harder to fall asleep.
- **Food**
  - **Healthy Snack Swap:** Swap out junk for tasty alternatives like apple slices with peanut butter or a yogurt parfait with granola and berries.
  - **DIY Smoothies:** Experiment with different smoothie recipes. Try blending spinach, banana, and almond milk for a tasty green smoothie!
  - **Eat the Rainbow:** Add color to your meals with different fruits and veggies. Aim to have at least three colors on your plate for every meal.
  - **Weekly Cooking Challenge:** Try cooking a new, healthy recipe each week. Get your friends involved and share your creations.
  - **Flavored Water:** Flavor your water with slices of lemon, cucumber, or strawberries.
- **Exercise**
  - **Playlist Power:** Create a high-energy playlist and have mini dance parties in your room. It's a fun way to get moving!
  - **TikTok Challenges:** Join in on the latest dance challenges and get your heart pumping.
  - **Explore Outdoors:** Plan a weekly hike, bike ride, or trip to the park with friends.

- **Sport Switch-Up:** Try a new sport or activity each month.
- **Active Gaming:** Play fitness video games, like Just Dance or Ring Fit Adventure, that get you moving.

Have you ever heard the saying, "Prevention is the best cure?" Being proactive about your health is an important adult skill that you can start cultivating during your teen years.

Understanding the Importance of Sleep

How much sleep do you get each night? Ideally, you should be getting 8–10 hours, but most teens get less sleep than they need.

Sleep is crucial, and those extra z's really can improve your life. Prioritizing sleep is a life hack you won't regret.

Remember, sleep is a necessity, not a luxury.

ADDRESSING COMMON SLEEP CHALLENGES

You'd think that sleep would be straightforward, but your teen body is going through a lot, which can shake things up in the sleep department.

3 Common Sleep Issues Among Teens

1. Insomnia

Insomnia is when you have trouble falling asleep, staying asleep, or both. It can leave you feeling tired and irritable during the day.

- **Causes:** Stress, anxiety, caffeine, and irregular sleep schedules are common culprits.
- **Solutions:** Create a relaxing bedtime routine, limit caffeine and sugar in the afternoon and evening, and manage stress with journaling, deep breathing, or meditation.

2. Irregular Sleep Patterns

Staying up late and sleeping in can disrupt your circadian rhythm.

- **Causes:** Homework, social activities, and screen time can all disrupt your sleep routine.
- **Solutions:** Keep a consistent sleep schedule, avoid late-afternoon naps, and get morning sunlight to help reset your circadian rhythm.

3. Difficulty Waking Up

Struggling to get out of bed in the morning can indicate that you are not getting enough quality sleep.

- **Causes:** Inconsistent bedtimes, late-night screen use, and not enough sleep.
- **Solutions:** Use a gradual alarm, develop an energizing morning routine, and maintain good sleep hygiene to ensure you get enough sleep.

If you've tried everything and still have trouble sleeping, it might be time to talk to a professional. You know your body. If something feels off, ask for help.

Health Really Is Wealth

Being healthy is more than exercising and eating right. Taking care of your body means taking pride in how you look and feel. Your mental health is just as vital as your physical health, helping you grow into your unique self.

COMMUNICATION

"The most important thing in communication is to hear
what isn't being said."
– Peter Drucker

Communication is one of the most valuable skills you can master, but it involves more than just words. If you've ever seen your friend grimace or tense up after you've said something unkind, you get it. Both verbal and non-verbal communication can greatly affect how your message is received and perceived.

Mastering Verbal and Non-Verbal Communication

Did you know that behavior is a form of communication? Your actions, gestures, and facial expressions often reflect an internal emotion. This means that when you speak to someone, you are telling them just as much by what you don't say as you do with the words you choose.

TIPS FOR CLEAR AND EFFECTIVE SPOKEN COMMUNICATION

Structure Your Ideas

Have a clear structure when speaking, especially in formal settings. Think of it as telling a story with a beginning, middle, and end. Start with a main point, add details, and conclude clearly. This keeps your listener engaged and makes your point clear. Structured communication is great for school presentations or interviews.

Keep It Simple and Clear

Be concise. If explaining something complicated, break it into smaller, easy-to-understand pieces. For example, when describing a math concept to a friend, use simple examples and go step-by-step.

Mind Your Tone, Pace, and Volume

How you say something can be just as important as what you say. Speak at a steady pace — not too fast and not too slow. Adjust your volume so everyone can hear you. Be mindful of your tone. If you sound bored or irritated, your audience will likely feel the same.

UNDERSTANDING THE ROLE OF BODY LANGUAGE AND TONE OF VOICE

Can you tell when your parents are mad just by the way they say your name? Tone and body language can sometimes tell you more about someone's feelings than words alone. Learning how to "read" people can make you a better friend and help you navigate social situations.

Body Language Matters

Your body language speaks volumes. Good posture (like standing up straight) shows confidence, while slouching can make you seem uninterested. Using your hands can emphasize points, but excessive gestures can be distracting.

Facial Expressions

Use your facial expressions to convey emotions. Smile when you're happy, and show concern when you're confused. Your expressions should match your words. If you say, "I'm so excited," but look bored, people will trust your face over your words.

Tone of Voice

Tone conveys more than words. A sarcastic "Nice job!" can sound insulting, while a warm "How are you?" can feel genuine. Ensure your tone matches your message to avoid misunderstandings.

PRACTICING AND IMPROVING COMMUNICATION SKILLS

Working on your communication skills can feel awkward, so some of these activities may not be for you. Try them out and pick the ones that make you feel comfortable:

Role-Playing:

- Practice different scenarios with friends or family.
- Try situations like job interviews, speeches, or resolving conflicts.
- Role-playing can feel embarrassing, so do it with people you trust.

Public Speaking Clubs:

- Join clubs like Toastmasters or a school debate team.
- Practice speaking in front of others and get feedback.
- Regular practice boosts confidence and improves skills.

Video Recording:

- Record yourself speaking on your phone or computer.
- Watch the playback to review body language, expressions, and tone.
- Identify nervous habits, like fidgeting or overusing "um."

Do a "Mirror Challenge." Stand in front of a mirror and say a positive affirmation. Not only will saying a positive affirmation help rewire your brain and improve your self-esteem, it will also help with your speaking skills.

Digital Communication and Etiquette

Have you ever stopped to think about how much of your communication happens on a device? Whether you're texting your friends, emailing a teacher, or posting on social media, it's important to understand the unique challenges and opportunities that come with communicating online.

THE UNIQUE ASPECTS OF DIGITAL COMMUNICATION

Digital communication has its own rules and challenges.

No Non-Verbal Cues

In face-to-face conversations, we rely heavily on body language, facial expressions, and tone of voice to understand each other. These cues help us gauge emotions and intentions, but they are missing in a text, email, or DM, often leading to misunderstandings. For example, a simple "OK" in a text can be interpreted as positive, neutral, or even sarcastic.

Permanence of Digital Communication

Once you hit send, your message is often out there for good. Unlike a spoken conversation that fades away, digital messages can be saved, shared, and referenced later. A hasty comment or an emotional outburst can have long-lasting consequences. The Internet has a long memory, so always think before posting.

TIPS FOR CONVEYING TONE AND INTENTION CLEARLY IN DIGITAL FORMATS

- **Use Emojis Wisely**: Emojis are a fun way to convey tone and emotions. A well-placed smiley face can soften a request or show your friend you aren't mad at them.
- **Consider Your Audience**: A text to a friend can be casual and include slang, while an email to a teacher should be more formal. Always start with a greeting and end with a sign-

off, like "Hi, Mr. Smith, I wanted to ask about the homework assignment. Thanks, Alex."

- **Proofread Before Sending**: Always read over your message before hitting send. This is especially important for emails or messages that many people could see. A typo can change the meaning of your message and create confusion, so also check that you are sending it to the right person.

MAINTAINING DIGITAL ETIQUETTE AND MANAGING DIGITAL FOOTPRINTS

In today's interconnected world, your digital footprint is here to stay. Whether you're texting friends, posting on social media, or engaging in online chat, how you behave online can have a lasting impact on your reputation and relationships.

Digital Etiquette: The Basics

- **Respect Others' Privacy**: Just because you can share something doesn't mean you should. Always get consent before posting pictures, tagging friends, or sharing personal information. What you share about someone else can affect their privacy and reputation.

- **Avoid Oversharing**: Be mindful of how much personal information you're putting online. Keep details like your home address, phone number, and current location private.

The Internet is a big place, and sharing too much can have dangerous consequences.

- **Be Kind and Considerate**: Treat others online as you would like to be treated. Arguing, trolling, or spreading negativity can be harmful and tend to spiral into something bigger and nastier. Remember, behind every screen is a real person with feelings.
- **Understand the Impact of Your Words**: Online words can be powerful. They can uplift and encourage, but they can also hurt and damage. Think before you type, and consider how others might receive your words. Spreading rumors or participating in cyberbullying can be more damaging than you know.

Managing Your Digital Footprint

- **Understand Your Digital Footprint**: Everything you do online leaves a trace. This includes posts, comments, likes, shares, and even the websites you visit. Future employers, colleges, and others can search and see your digital footprint.
- **Think Before You Post:** Once something is out there, it can be challenging to remove it. Think about the long-term impact of your posts. Will this be something you'll be proud of years from now? Avoid posting in the heat of the moment or when you're feeling emotional.

- **Use Privacy Settings:** Most social media platforms offer privacy settings that allow you to control who sees your posts. Use these settings to keep your personal information and posts visible only to people you trust.
- **Clean Up Your Online Presence:** Review your old posts, comments, and photos periodically. Delete anything that no longer represents who you are or that could be seen as inappropriate. This is especially important before applying for jobs or college. If you wouldn't want your grandma to see it, should it be online?

Maintaining good digital etiquette and managing your digital footprint helps create a positive and respectful online presence. This not only helps protect your privacy and reputation, but also ensures that your online interactions won't make you cringe years later.

The Importance of Active Listening and Clear Expression

Have you heard of active listening? It is a skill that can transform your interactions now and as you enter adulthood.

Think of active listening as listening in 3D. You don't just hear the words someone is saying. In addition, you see their body language and understand the meaning and emotion beneath their words.

TECHNIQUES FOR ACTIVE LISTENING

Active listening involves being present in the conversation, showing empathy, and responding thoughtfully. When you actively listen to someone, you build trust and strengthen connections.

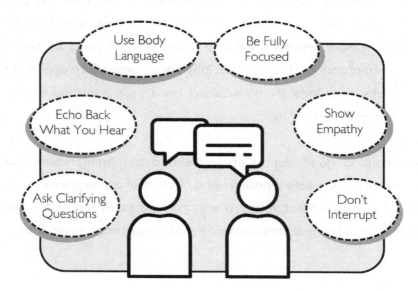

Give Your Full Attention

When someone is speaking, put away distractions like your phone or the TV and be fully present. Make eye contact to show you're engaged and interested.

Reflect Back What You Hear

Paraphrase or summarize what is said to show that you understand. This also gives the other person a chance to clarify or explain more, which can help you understand better.

Top Tip

Use phrases like "What I'm hearing is..." or "It sounds like you're saying..." For example, if a friend says, "I had a rough day at school because I forgot my homework," you might respond, "So, you're feeling stressed because you left your homework at home?"

Ask Clarifying Questions

Ask questions if you need clarification. This shows that you're interested and want to understand their perspective fully. Questions like "Can you tell me more about that?" or "What happened next?" can help you dig deeper.

Use Non-Verbal Cues

Your body language can say a lot. Nodding, leaning slightly forward, and maintaining eye contact shows you're engaged. Avoid crossing your arms or looking around, as these can make you seem disinterested.

Avoid Interrupting

Nothing breaks the active listening spell like interrupting. Let the speaker finish their thoughts before you jump in. Interrupting can frustrate the speaker and disrupt the flow of the conversation.

Show Empathy

When in doubt, aim for empathy. A huge part of active listening is being present with respect and understanding. When you try to understand the speaker's feelings and perspective, you show them they are valued. For example, if a friend is upset about a bad grade, you might say, "I can see why you're upset. That sounds really frustrating."

ENCOURAGING RESPECT IN CONVERSATIONS

Respect in communication means treating others with consideration and valuing their opinions, even if you disagree.

- **Use Polite Language:** Words like "please," "thank you," and "excuse me" can greatly influence how your message is received. Being respectful and polite often helps you achieve your goals without any extra cost.

- **Avoid Interrupting:** Let the other person finish speaking before you respond. This shows respect for their right to express themselves and allows you to fully assess the situation before engaging.
- **Stay Calm:** Even if the conversation becomes heated, try to remain calm and composed. Raising your voice or getting angry can escalate the situation and make respectful communication difficult.
- **Be Open-Minded:** Be willing to consider other viewpoints and change your mind when you learn new information. Being honest and respectful is more important than being right.

You Are Always Communicating

Everything you do or say is a form of communication. Every smile, frown, text, DM, and eye roll sends a message. Learning how to manage your verbal and non-verbal communication will help you get ahead in life and make you a better friend. As Peter Drucker says, "The most important thing in communication is to hear what isn't being said."

10

LOVE

"Being deeply loved by someone gives you strength,
while loving someone deeply gives you courage."
— Lao Tzu

Love isn't just one thing—it's a kaleidoscope of emotions, connections, and experiences that shape who we are and how we relate to others.

Each form of love brings something different to your life, teaches you something new, and helps you grow. They all come with ups and downs, pain and pleasure. But that is what makes love such a beautiful experience and one you should cherish.

The Different Types of Love

From the comforting warmth of familial love to the excitement of a new romance, each type of love brings something unique to our lives. Exploring these forms of love helps you understand yourself and others better.

Love helps you build stronger and more fulfilling relationships. Whether it's the loyal support of a best friend or a deep bond with a family member, different forms of love bring richness to your life.

DISCUSSING DIFFERENT TYPES OF LOVE

Love isn't just about romance and fairy tales — it's a complex and multifaceted emotion that comes in various forms. Nurturing each type of relationship requires effort and understanding, whether with family, friends, or a romantic partner.

Familial Love

Familial love is affection for parents, siblings, and other family members. It's often the first kind of love you experience, and shapes your understanding of relationships.

- **Characteristics:** Unconditional, nurturing, protective.

- **Examples:** Think about how your parents or guardians care for you when you're sick, or how your siblings might annoy you one minute but stand up for you the next. It's those Sunday dinners, family vacations, and even the little arguments that make up familial love.

Top Tip

Show appreciation for your family by doing small acts of kindness, like helping out with chores without being asked or simply spending quality time together. These gestures strengthen familial bonds and show that you value your relationships with your family members.

Platonic Love

Platonic love is what you share with your close friends. It's about companionship, shared interests, and mutual respect.

- **Characteristics:** Trust, loyalty, shared experiences.
- **Examples:** Remember that friend who always has your back, no matter what? Or the one who knows what to say to cheer you up? Platonic love is all about those late-night conversations, inside jokes, and being there for each other through thick and thin.

Top Tip

Keep your platonic relationships strong by being a good listener, making time for your friends, and showing appreciation for their presence in your life.

Romantic Love

Romantic love is the passionate and intimate connection you share with a partner. It's the butterflies-in-your-stomach feeling, the excitement of discovering someone new, and the deep bond that grows over time.

- **Characteristics:** Attraction, passion, intimacy.
- **Examples:** Think about the excitement of a first date, the joy of finding common interests, or the comfort of a long-term relationship. Romantic love can be thrilling and sometimes challenging, but it's an important aspect of many people's lives.

Navigating Teenage Crushes and First Relationships

Your first crush is a significant step in your teen journey. You might not know it now, but few things match the energy and emotion of your first crush or relationship. They bring a whirlwind of emotions that can be both thrilling and overwhelming.

UNDERSTANDING THE EMOTIONAL ASPECTS OF CRUSHES AND RELATIONSHIPS

Crushes can hit hard. It's normal to feel like your heart races whenever you see or think about your crush. Your feelings are real and important, but they can also change quickly. Emotions during a crush or first relationship can be unpredictable. One moment, you're on cloud nine; the next, you're anxious or unsure. This is all part of the process.

Navigating First Relationships

- **Communication Is Key:** Open and honest communication helps prevent misunderstandings. Discuss your feelings, listen to your partner, and talk about what you both want from the relationship.
- **Setting Boundaries:** Establish and respect emotional and physical boundaries. Discuss what you're comfortable with, and respect each other's limits. Healthy boundaries make relationships stronger.
- **Maintaining Individuality:** While spending time together is great, remember who you are. Keep up with your hobbies and

friends, and ensure you have some "me time." It's important to grow as individuals, as well as a couple.

- **Staying Grounded:** It's okay to feel deeply, but try to maintain a balanced perspective. Not every crush or relationship will last forever, and that's perfectly normal.
- **Getting Advice:** Don't hesitate to talk to trusted friends or family about your feelings. They can offer valuable insights and support. Remember to keep an open mind.
- **Enjoying the Journey:** Relationships are learning experiences. Enjoy the good times, learn from the challenges, and grow from each experience.

Understanding and managing the emotional aspects of crushes and relationships allows you to enjoy these experiences while staying balanced and true to yourself. Embrace the highs and lows and remember that each step is a valuable part of growing up.

Build healthy romantic relationships by communicating openly and respecting each other's boundaries. Remember, it's important to maintain your individuality while growing closer to someone else.

Dealing with the Complexities and Emotions of Heartbreak

Heartbreak is tough. It can feel like the world has turned upside down, and you might wonder how you'll ever feel okay again. It's an all-consuming feeling that, while painful to experience, is entirely normal.

COPING WITH HEARTBREAK

The advice below may seem obvious, but that doesn't make it any less true. It may not feel helpful when your heart is hurting, and there is no "right" way to go through a heartbreak, but take the advice that resonates and leave the rest until you feel ready for it.

- **Embrace Your Emotions:** It's okay to feel sad, angry, or confused. Allow yourself to experience these emotions instead of bottling them up. Cry if you need to, talk it out with someone you trust, or write your feelings down.
- **Prioritize Self-Care:** Heartbreak can take a toll on your physical and mental health. Take care of yourself by eating well, staying hydrated, getting enough sleep, and doing things that make you feel good. Self-care isn't just about pampering yourself — it's about nurturing your well-being.
- **Seek Support:** Talk to friends, family, or a counselor about what you're going through. Surround yourself with people

who care about you and can offer comfort and perspective. Knowing someone is there for you can make a huge difference.

- **Give Yourself Time:** Healing takes time, and there's no set timeline for moving on. Be patient and allow yourself the space to heal at your own pace. Remember, it's okay not to be okay for a while.

STRATEGIES FOR MOVING FORWARD

- **Focus on Personal Growth:** Use this time to rediscover yourself, especially if you had a relationship that seemed to "consume" you. Dive into hobbies, explore new interests, or set personal goals. Channeling your energy into self-improvement can be incredibly empowering.
- **Reflect and Learn:** Consider what you've learned from the relationship and the breakup. What worked? What didn't? Understanding these lessons can help you in future relationships.
- **Create New Routines:** Establishing new routines can help you break free from old habits associated with your past relationship. Start a new hobby, join a club, or volunteer. Keeping busy can help you move forward.
- **Stay Positive:** It's easy to dwell on the negatives, but try to focus on the positives. Focus on gratitude whenever possible. It's easier to get over a broken heart when you notice everything good in your life.

The Importance of Respect, Consent, and Healthy Relationship Dynamics

Respect and consent are essential for healthy relationship dynamics. To build strong, positive connections with others, you need the right tools.

Respect forms the foundation of all relationships, while consent ensures that interactions are based on mutual agreement and understanding. Learning about these principles helps you form meaningful relationships and grow as a person.

CONSENT AND RESPECTFUL COMMUNICATION

Consent is vital in every interaction, whether it's physical, emotional, or conversational. It means everyone involved is comfortable with what's happening, without feeling pressured. Consent must be enthusiastic and ongoing, and should be able to be withdrawn at any time. It's about respecting each other's boundaries and ensuring everyone feels safe. Remember, you can always change your mind. Everyone should feel happy with what's happening.

CONSENT is

EXPLICIT	NO always means NO	DIRECT
Clearly expressed via words or actions	Only YES means YES	Communicated clearly and directly

AWARE	ONGOING
Fully known, not impaired by drugs or alcohol	Reaffirmed at each stage of sexual activity

MUTUAL	CLEARLY STATED
All participants agree willingly and voluntarily	Never assumed based on actions like clothing, alcohol use, or dancing

Any sexual interactions must occur between consenting adults.

Example of Consent:

Imagine you're planning a group outing with friends to see a movie. One friend suggests a horror film, but you're not comfortable with scary movies. You speak up and say, "I'm not really into horror films. How about we watch a comedy, instead?" Your friends respect your preference and agree to watch a comedy. This shows how expressing your boundaries allows everyone to make choices that everyone feels comfortable with.

COMMUNICATING BOUNDARIES

Understanding and respecting boundaries is crucial for consent. When you talk about your boundaries, you express what's okay and what's not, while also listening to others' comfort levels. In relationships, this might mean discussing what feels right and paying attention to non-verbal cues.

Example of Communicating Boundaries:

Imagine you have a close friend who likes to borrow your things without asking. You feel uncomfortable, because they don't always return items promptly or in good condition. To communicate your boundaries, you might say, "Hey, I've noticed you borrow my stuff a lot. I'm okay with that sometimes, but I'd appreciate it if you could ask me first. It's important for me to know where my things are and to keep them in good shape."

RESPECTFUL COMMUNICATION

Respectful communication builds trust and understanding in relationships. It involves actively listening when someone talks, being honest but kind in your responses, and considering how your words and actions affect others. This approach ensures that everyone feels valued and heard, creating a space where respect and understanding thrive.

Example of Respectful Communication:

Suppose your friend shares something personal with you. Instead of interrupting or offering advice right away, you listen attentively and ask questions to better understand their feelings. You respond with empathy and avoid judgment, showing that you value their thoughts and feelings. This kind of communication builds trust and strengthens your bond by respecting their emotions and experiences.

RECOGNIZING SIGNS OF HEALTHY VS. UNHEALTHY RELATIONSHIPS

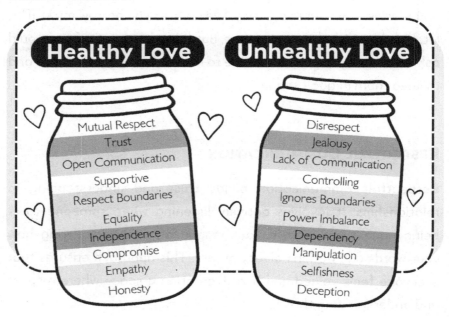

Healthy Love	Unhealthy Love
Mutual Respect	Disrespect
Trust	Jealousy
Open Communication	Lack of Communication
Supportive	Controlling
Respect Boundaries	Ignores Boundaries
Equality	Power Imbalance
Independence	Dependency
Compromise	Manipulation
Empathy	Selfishness
Honesty	Deception

New relationships often bring intense emotions that can cloud your judgment. It's easy to get caught up in the excitement of new feelings, making it hard to recognize the warning signs of an unhealthy relationship, whether in friendships or romantic partnerships.

In a healthy relationship, you can be yourself without fear of being judged. You and your friend or partner respect each other's feelings and boundaries. For example, if you're having a bad day, they listen and try to help.

Unhealthy relationships can feel stressful or even scary. Signs of an unhealthy relationship might include feeling pressured to do things you're not comfortable with, like skipping class or going against your values. Perhaps your partner or friend tries to control who you hang out with or makes you feel bad about yourself.

If you're in an unhealthy relationship, it's okay to ask for help. Talk to someone you trust, like a parent, teacher, or counselor. They can help you figure out what to do next to stay safe and feel better. You deserve to be in relationships that make you feel good about yourself, and where you're treated with respect.

Love Really Does Make the World Go Round

Understanding love and relationships is a rite of passage everyone goes through. Whether familial, platonic, or romantic, these connections shape who you are, who you become, and how you interact with the world.

Healthy relationships are built on respect, trust, and open communication. It's okay to seek support if you find yourself in a situation that doesn't feel right. By valuing yourself and others, you're building strong foundations for creating lasting relationships.

CONCLUSION

That's it! We've covered a lot of ground, and you should be proud of yourself for completing this journey. From mastering study habits and understanding different types of love to developing effective communication skills and maintaining good health and hygiene, you've gained valuable insights and tools.

Think about how much you've learned and grown. This book is just the beginning, a stepping stone toward becoming a well-rounded, capable individual. Keep practicing what you've learned and continue to hone those skills. When life happens (and it does... all the time), you'll be glad to have these skills up your sleeve.

Remember, learning is a continuous process. Stay curious and open-minded, and seek new experiences and opportunities for growth — even when it's challenging. As Neil deGrasse Tyson said, "The day we stop exploring is the day we commit ourselves to live in a stagnant world, devoid of curiosity, empty of dreams." Whether it's picking up a new hobby or seeking advice from mentors, keep pushing yourself to grow.

One of the most rewarding things you can do with your newfound knowledge is to share it with others. Help your friends, younger siblings, or anyone who might benefit from what you've learned. Live out these lessons by showing empathy and practicing clear communication. By supporting each other, you create a stronger, more connected community.

You're not alone on this journey. You've got the tools you need to navigate the challenges and opportunities ahead. Remember, learning is a lifelong journey, and each step you take brings you closer to becoming the best version of you.

Here's to your continued growth and success. Keep pushing forward, stay positive, and don't hesitate to revisit this book whenever you need a boost.

You've got this!

Your friend, Ferne.

THANKS
FOR READING MY
BOOK!

I truly hope you enjoyed the book and that the content is valuable now and in the future.

I would be grateful if you could leave an honest review or a star rating on Amazon.
(A star rating is just a couple of clicks away.)

By leaving a review, you'll help other parents discover this valuable resource for their children. Thank you!

To leave a review & help spread the word

SCAN HERE

APPENDIX

1. Azab, M., PhD. (2020, March 11). Research shows slow connections between logical and emotional brain parts. *Psychology Today*. https://www.psychologytoday.com/za/blog/neuroscience-in-everyday-life/201810/why-are-teens-so-emotional
2. Ba, M. R. C. (2024, March 18). *The neuroscience of gratitude and effects on the brain*. PositivePsychology.com. https://positivepsychology.com/neuroscience-of-gratitude/
3. Chen, L. (2023). Influence of music on the hearing and mental health of adolescents and countermeasures. *Frontiers in Neuroscience*, 17. https://doi.org/10.3389/fnins.2023.1236638
4. Dodgson, L. (2017, March 29). *How 10 highly successful people manage stress*. Business Insider. https://www.businessinsider.com/how-successful-people-deal-with-stress-2017-3#4-warren-buffet-4
5. Doherty, R., Madigan, S., Nevill, A., Warrington, G., & Ellis, J. G. (2023). The impact of kiwifruit consumption on the sleep and recovery of elite athletes. *Nutrients*, *15*(10), 2274. https://doi.org/10.3390/nu15102274
6. *First impressions*. (2024, February 16). Psychology Today. https://www.psychologytoday.com/us/basics/first-impressions
7. Illa, J. (2024, April 1). *Teen Skin Health: Acne, Hormones, and Skincare Tips | Children's Skin Center PA*. Children's Skin Center PA. https://www.childrensskincenter.com/2024/01/12/teen-skin-health-acne-hormones-and-skincare-tips/
8. Kircanski, K., Lieberman, M. D., & Craske, M. G. (2012). Feelings into words. *Psychological Science*, *23*(10), 1086–1091. https://doi.org/10.1177/0956797612443830

9. P, E. (2020, July 30). How Many Times Do You Touch Your Face? Here's What Scientists Have to Say. *Science Times*. https://www. sciencetimes.com/articles/26685/20200730/many-times-touch-face-scientists-answer.htm

10. *Relationships improve your odds of survival by 50 percent, research finds.* (2010, July 10). ScienceDaily. https://www.sciencedaily.com/ releases/2010/07/100727174909.htm

11. Rutkowski, D., & Hastedt, D. (n.d.). *Kids with a desk and a quiet place to study do better in school, data shows.* The Conversation. https:// theconversation.com/kids-with-a-desk-and-a-quiet-place-to-study-do-better-in-school-data-shows-159680

12. *Stress relief from laughter? It's no joke.* (2023, September 22). Mayo Clinic. https://www.mayoclinic.org/healthy-lifestyle/stress-management/in-depth/stress-relief/art-20044456

13. Success. (2024). In *Merriam-Webster Dictionary*. https://www.merriam-webster.com/dictionary/success#:~:text=%3A%20favorable%20 or%20desired%20outcome,%3A%20one%20that%20succeeds

14. Suni, E., & Suni, E. (2023, October 4). *Teens and sleep*. Sleep Foundation. https://www.sleepfoundation.org/teens-and-sleep

15. Teens and sleep: Why you need it and how to get enough. (2008). *Paediatrics & Child Health*, *13*(1), 69–70. https://doi.org/10.1093/ pch/13.1.69

16. Ware, S. (2024, May 14). Here's why teens' body odor can be especially strong. *Science News Explores*. https://www.snexplores.org/article/teen-body-odor-smell-chemistry

17. *What are some myths about sleep?* (2019, April 29). https://www.nichd. nih.gov/. https://www.nichd.nih.gov/health/topics/sleep/conditioninfo/ sleep-myths

18. Young, L. (2020, February 7). *Is your cell phone really 10 times dirtier than a toilet seat?* https://www.ualberta.ca/public-health/news/2017/ september/is-your-cell-phone-really-10-times-dirtier-than-a-toilet-seat.html

Made in the USA
Coppell, TX
22 December 2024

43380216R00105